IT'S ELEMENTARY!
TWELVE SHORT PLAYS FOR
UPPER ELEMENTARY SCHOOL ACTORS

---

by Nicole B. Adkins, Robin Blasberg, Rachel Bublitz,
Matt Buchanan, Catherine Castellani, Annie Harrison
Elliott, Claudia Haas, Arthur M. Jolly, Laura King,
Meredith Dayna Levy, Anne Negri
and Isabella Russell-Ides

Curated by Nicole B. Adkins and Jonathan Dorf

www.youthplays.com
info@youthplays.com
424-703-5315

COPYRIGHT RULES TO REMEMBER

1. To produce this play, you must receive prior written permission from YouthPLAYS and pay the required royalty.

2. You must pay a royalty each time the play is performed in the presence of audience members outside of the cast and crew. Royalties are due whether or not admission is charged, whether or not the play is presented for profit, for charity or for educational purposes, or whether or not anyone associated with the production is being paid.

3. No changes, including cuts or additions, are permitted to the script without written prior permission from YouthPLAYS.

4. Do not copy this book or any part of it without written permission from YouthPLAYS.

5. Credit to the author and YouthPLAYS is required on all programs and other promotional items associated with this play's performance.

When you pay royalties, you are recognizing the hard work that went into creating the play and making a statement that a play is something of value. We think this is important, and we hope that everyone will do the right thing, thus allowing playwrights to generate income and continue to create wonderful new works for the stage.

Plays are owned by the playwrights who wrote them. Violating a playwright's copyright is a very serious matter and violates both United States and international copyright law. Infringement is punishable by actual damages and attorneys' fees, statutory damages of up to $150,000 per incident, and even possible criminal sanctions. **Infringement is theft. Don't do it.**

Have a question about copyright? Please contact us by email at info@youthplays.com or by phone at 424-703-5315. When in doubt, please ask.

FOREWORD

It's Elementary! was born out of a desire to fill what we recognized as a real need for quality, age-appropriate opportunities for younger actors. Upper elementary students deserve compelling scripts about which they can get excited—scripts that can help them fall in love with the stage and the imaginative worlds it creates. At the same time, we know their teachers need plays that are flexible enough to work on stage and in the classroom, and that can fit a range of needs and abilities: plays with large and flexible-sized casts with choral, participatory opportunities, as well as smaller cast shows with more challenging roles for burgeoning thespians.

With this in mind, we reached out to playwrights who had experience working with and writing for and about this age group, but also welcomed others who wrote excellent plays for older performers and were enthusiastic about taking on a new challenge. One of the things that excited us most about the work we received was not only that many scripts fit the bill in terms of our goals, but that they were all so different! We are even now in the midst of planning a second volume.

Whether you have a large group or a smaller one, experienced actors or beginners, and regardless of your gender breakdown, you'll find good options—and in a wide array of styles and genres—for your classroom, for performance or anything in between. To maximize their flexibility, these plays can be licensed individually or in a group, in which case they can be used in any order and with any titles omitted to suit your needs.

So if you've been wrestling with the riddle of where to find plays for your group, we have the answer. In fact, *It's Elementary!*

> —Nicole B. Adkins and Jonathan Dorf

THE PLAYS

ABOUT THE COLLECTION

These plays may be performed individually or grouped in any combination to create a show of the desired length and performed as **It's Elementary!**. To do every play in the collection requires 12+ performers. For smaller groups, however, it's possible to perform more than half of the plays with casts of 8 or fewer. If each role is played by a different actor, there are opportunities for over 100 performers.

Plays may occasionally include [bracketed] dialogue which may be substituted for the original dialogue as needed.

ACKNOWLEDGMENT

Special thanks to Laura King for all her work reading, dramaturging and helping to shape this collection.

NO TALKING ALLOWED!
by Rachel Bublitz

CAST OF CHARACTERS

MRS./MR. COHEN, any gender, teacher, 30s+, strict. Wears bifocals.

JORDAN, any gender. Just trying to take a test the only way they know how.

PENCIL*

SNAKE*

FROG*

DESK*

AARON, any gender. A hall monitor. They sleep in their hall monitor sash.

LOCKER*

CUSTODIAN MEG/MOE, any gender, 20s+.

MOP*

BIFOCALS*

PRINCIPAL LOPEZ, any gender, 40s+. Makes all the rules.

*THESE CHARACTERS CAN BE PUPPETS, ACTORS IN COSTUME, AN OFFSTAGE VOICE AND/OR ANY OF THESE TECHNIQUES COMBINED.

PRODUCTION NOTE

This is a fast-paced, silly ten-minute play. To keep it moving, I recommend using suggested set and props; a big part of theatre is, after all, letting your audience use their imagination. A simple way this could be accomplished: posters or writing on a white/chalk board announcing various locations, and actors wearing signs around their necks to tell the audience what "object" they are. Feel free to come up with other creative ways to get this information to your audience. Have fun.

For Alex

(A science classroom. There are a few animals in cages — a SNAKE, a FROG, etc. — desks, chairs, and other classroom accessories. MRS. COHEN enters dragging JORDAN by the arm or ear.)

MRS. COHEN: That's the last straw! There is NO TALKING ALLOWED during TESTS! I have told you this! REPEATEDLY!

JORDAN: But I'm not talking to other people, honest — I'm reading the test out loud just to myself! It helps me understand the questions and —

MRS. COHEN: You are distracting your fellow students and it is unacceptable! You will sit in here until your peers are finished, and you will get a ZERO on today's test!

JORDAN: No! Please! I studied! Maybe you could let me finish in here — that way I won't disturb anyone and I can take the test the way that helps me —

MRS. COHEN: I'm not falling for that old trick. You think I was born yesterday?

JORDAN: It's not a trick, I promise —

MRS. COHEN: Likely story. Now you know the drill: sit and zip it!

(Jordan sits. Mrs. Cohen exits. Jordan taps PENCIL. Through the next lines the tapping becomes more frenzied:)

JORDAN: What is wrong with me? Why can't I just talk *inside* my head like a normal person? I'm failing this test, and if I can't get it together I'm going to fail all future tests, and then I'm going to be stuck in summer school or — *(Gasps.)* Repeating this whole grade! NOOOOO! And then I'll never go to college or have a job or — *(Flips Pencil across the room.)* THAT WAS AN ACCIDENT! I SWEAR I'M NOT A JUVENILE DELINQUENT!

(Jordan rushes over and picks up Pencil.)

PENCIL: You need to take it down a notch, kid—you're going to give yourself a heart attack!

(Jordan freezes, looks around.)

JORDAN: ...Who said that?

PENCIL: Your long and pointed pal, of course!

(Jordan looks under desks and behind the animal enclosures. Jordan sees a Snake.)

JORDAN: (*Moving closer to the Snake's cage:*) Did...Did you just talk to me?

FROG: You been watchin' too many of those wizard movies! The snake didn't talk to you, it was your pencil!

JORDAN: My pencil?!?

(Jordan looks closer at Pencil.)

PENCIL: Hi friend! Now as I was saying, you've got to relax a little, breathe in, breathe out. I think if we put our heads together we can figure out a way to get your teacher to understand—

(Jordan drops Pencil.)

JORDAN: AHHHHH!

PENCIL: Again? That really hurts, you know!

FROG: Yeah, pretty rude to toss someone on the floor, dude. Especially when that someone is just tryin' to help you.

(Jordan backs away from Frog and Pencil.)

JORDAN: But— But— But— But— But— Frogs can't talk! And neither can pencils!

(Jordan bumps into DESK.)

DESK: Hey! Watch it, buddy!

(Jordan jumps into the air, screeches and runs. The science room becomes a hallway with a LOCKER on the wall. Jordan runs through the hallway and smashes straight into AARON, a hall monitor who has a good shot at becoming the most rule-abiding hall monitor in the history of hall monitors. Jordan and Aaron both fall to the floor. Jordan gets back up and tries to run away.)

AARON: I don't think so. Not on my watch, buddy.

(Aaron tackles Jordan, then sits on top of Jordan and pulls out a walkie-talkie, a walkie-talkie they brought from home to be even more efficient at hall monitoring.)

(Into walkie-talkie:) Got a runner.

JORDAN: No, no! No! You gotta let me go, this pencil —

AARON: Save it for the vice principal.

JORDAN: YOU HAVE TO LISTEN TO ME! I— I was taking a test and I got kicked out for talking —

AARON: Figures.

JORDAN: LET ME FINISH! I was in the science room, ALONE, and all of a sudden my pencil was telling me to calm down and then a frog said to me I wasn't a wizard, and a desk yelled at me and— And— And— And so I ran!

AARON: *(Into walkie-talkie:)* Yeah, we're gonna need to take a urine sample on this one.

LOCKER: Hush your mouth! You'd be spooked too if a pencil talked to you!

(Beat.)

AARON: RUN FOR YOUR LIFE!

AARON & JORDAN: AHHHHHHHHHHHHHHHHHHH!

(Aaron and Jordan get up and run together. They run into CUSTODIAN MEG, who is in the middle of mopping with MOP. They all slip and slide.)

CUSTODIAN MEG: What do you two THINK YOU'RE DOING? YOU NEARLY KILLED ME!

AARON: You don't understand!

JORDAN: We're in danger!

AARON: DANGEROUS DANGER!

JORDAN: There's no time— My pencil— IT TALKED! And then a frog, and then a desk—

AARON: Yeah, and I was like, "Oh, you're crazy!" And I was about to drag Jordan to detention but a locker—MADE OF METAL—told me to hush up!

JORDAN: And now we're running for our lives.

CUSTODIAN MEG: I don't like practical jokes. Nope. Not one bit. Expected more from you, Aaron. I'm going to have to tell the principal. You don't deserve that sash!

(Aaron clings to the hall monitor sash as if their life depended on it.)

MOP: Can't you cut them a bit of slack? It's not everyday you come upon a talking pencil.

(Beat.)

CUSTODIAN MEG: Did— Did— Did— Did— Did that mop just talk to me?

JORDAN: Yep.

AARON: Sure did.

CUSTODIAN MEG: What do we do now?

JORDAN: We've been running and screaming in complete terror.

CUSTODIAN MEG: Sounds about right!

(Custodian Meg, Jordan and Aaron run away together.)

CUSTODIAN MEG, JORDAN & AARON: AHHHHHHHHHHHHHHHHHHHHHHHHHHHHHHHHHHHHHHHHH!

CUSTODIAN MEG: WHERE ARE WE EVEN GOING?

JORDAN: AS FAR AS OUR LEGS WILL TAKE US!

(Jordan, Aaron and Custodian Meg turn a corner and mow down Mrs. Cohen, who is wearing BIFOCALS. All are knocked to the floor.)

MRS. COHEN: JORDAN! What is going on? I was just checking on you and I discovered you are NOT WHERE I LEFT YOU!

JORDAN: You went to the science room? Did you notice anything?... Anything funny?

MRS. COHEN: Other than you missing? Nothing. Now help me up and explain yourself!

(Jordan gives Mrs. Cohen a hand up.)

JORDAN: I was at the place, the room, the science room, like you told me to be, and I was freaking out because my life was over because I failed that test when my pencil TALKED and said it'd help me brainstorm a way to get you to understand and then the frog and a desk joined in, so I ran as fast as I could —

AARON: And when I saw a kid running through the hall, I was like, they should get detention, but when I didn't believe the story a locker scolded me —

CUSTODIAN MEG: Then these two knocked ME DOWN, right in the middle of mopping, telling me this nutty story about talking pencils and frogs, and desks, and LOCKERS, and I was about to take them to call their parents when my mop told me to cut them some slack.

JORDAN: And now we're running for our lives.

MRS. COHEN: Of all the insane, dopey, foolish tricks I've heard over the years, this takes the cake! Aaron, I thought you respected your role as a hall monitor too much to get caught up in such a ridiculous crowd. And Custodian Meg! I am especially disappointed in you! You're an adult AND you should know better than to get caught up in the students' antics! As for *you* Jordan, I can't say I'm surprised. This incident will go down on your permanent record!

BIFOCALS: That's right! Give them all detention! They nearly broke me in half! Running in the halls WILL NOT BE TOLERATED! Isn't that right, Mrs. Cohen?

MRS. COHEN: ...

BIFOCALS: Mrs. Cohen?

MRS. COHEN: (*Whispering:*) Who said that?

> (*Jordan points to BIFOCALS. Mrs. Cohen slowly takes off Bifocals and turns them so she's looking at the front of them.*)

BIFOCALS: Good afternoon!

> (*Mrs. Cohen drops Bifocals and runs.*)

MRS. COHEN: AHHHHHHHHHHHHHHHHHHHHHHHH HHHHHHHHHHHHHHHHHH!

JORDAN: Shall we?

AARON: After you....

> (*Jordan, Aaron and Custodian Meg run after Mrs. Cohen.*)

CUSTODIAN MEG, JORDAN & AARON: AHHHHHHHHHHHHHHHHHHHHHHHHHHHHHHHHHHH HHHHHHHHHH!

(Mrs. Cohen, Jordan, Aaron and Custodian Meg run. The hall becomes the principal's office. A large desk is now on stage with PRINCIPAL LOPEZ sitting at it. The four runners barrel into the desk, knocking the office into a state of disarray. Principal Lopez climbs out from under the desk.)

PRINCIPAL LOPEZ: WHAT ON EARTH IS GOING ON?!

(Mrs. Cohen, Jordan, Aaron and Custodian Meg are all too out of breath to speak. Jordan holds up a finger indicating that they need a minute.)

I AM WAITING!

JORDAN: It's like this—

MRS. COHEN: Jordan was disrupting the whole class during a test—

JORDAN: I was JUST reading the questions out loud to myself! It helps—

MRS. COHEN: Do not interrupt your teacher! As I was saying, I took Jordan to the science room while everyone else finished the test and, well...

JORDAN: ...And there my pencil... It *talked* to me.

MRS. COHEN: And that's not it!

JORDAN: No! Then a frog chimed in, and a desk!

AARON: And when I tried to take Jordan to detention, a locker talked to me!

CUSTODIAN MEG: Then my mop talked to me!

MRS. COHEN: And last, but not least, my bifocals scolded them for running in the hall.

(Silence.)

PRINCIPAL LOPEZ: ...I don't know what to say.

JORDAN: It must be some sort of a phenomenon or something!

AARON: Or aliens!

CUSTODIAN MEG: Or ghosts!

MRS. COHEN: OR THE DEVIL!!!!!!!

PRINCIPAL LOPEZ: THAT IS ENOUGH! Phenomena, and aliens, and ghosts, and DEVILS are NOT allowed at this school! Do you hear me?... DO YOU HEAR ME?

MRS. COHEN, CUSTODIAN MEG, JORDAN & AARON: Yes! BUT—

PRINCIPAL LOPEZ: ZIP THOSE MOUTHS! If those things are not allowed, then those things are not allowed. I am the principal and I make all the rules. NOW! As for the talking during a test—

JORDAN: I promise, I was just reading the questions out loud—

PRINCIPAL LOPEZ: It seems to me the only solution is to let Jordan take the test in an empty classroom. That way the other students won't be disturbed.

JORDAN: THAT'S WHAT I'VE BEEN TRYING TO SAY!

PRINCIPAL LOPEZ: Great, then that's all settled. And now, unless there's something else unrelated to things talking that have no business talking, I suggest you all leave my office immediately and return to your various duties.

MRS. COHEN, CUSTODIAN MEG, JORDAN & AARON: Yes, Principal Lopez.

(With their heads down, Mrs. Cohen, Custodian Meg and Aaron exit. Jordan hangs back.)

PRINCIPAL LOPEZ: What are you waiting for?

JORDAN: ...I just, I...I thought—

PRINCIPAL LOPEZ: Spit it out!

JORDAN: ...I just thought something in here would pipe up, but I guess... (*Sighs.*) I guess not this time.

PRINCIPAL LOPEZ: Why don't you give me a hand with my desk?

(Jordan and Principal Lopez put the office back in order.)

I get stressed out over tests too. So I understand a little, but you've got to stop making up crazy stories about talking objects! I can't have all the students and staff running around scared to death—we'd never get any work done!

JORDAN: But I wasn't making any of it up! My pencil really did—

(Pencil rolls in.)

PENCIL: Principal Lopez!

(Jordan's mouth drops open.)

PRINCIPAL LOPEZ: Pencil! How are you? It's been ages!

PENCIL: I'm fine, but Jordan needs your help! Mrs. Cohen—

PRINCIPAL LOPEZ: If this is about the trouble with the test, don't worry! We worked all that out.

PENCIL: You're telling me I rolled all the way over here for nothing?

PRINCIPAL LOPEZ: Don't worry about it, it'll give us a chance to catch up. You want a coffee? Tea?

PENCIL: You got any Earl Grey?

PRINCIPAL LOPEZ: One Earl Grey coming up... Better get back to class, Jordan! Got that test to get back to, don't you?

JORDAN: Yeah, right... The...the test....

(Jordan carefully walks around Pencil and exits at a run.)

PRINCIPAL LOPEZ: Cream? Sugar?

PENCIL: No cream, two sugars, please and thank you.

(End of play.)

The Author Speaks

What inspired you to write this play?

I was inspired by the lack of listening I see in the world, and that I am also often guilty of myself. I think this is especially true when it comes to children; adults often don't take the time to really hear them. A lot of children's theater I've seen or read falls into the trope of adults teaching children lessons, and while I think this is fine and valid, I also strongly believe that children have a lot to teach us as well. With this play I wanted to give the children's voices authority as well. I wanted their characters not to be brushed off for "just being kids."

Was the structure or other elements of the play influenced by any other work?

Yes! This play was influenced heavily by an African folk story called *Talk*. I have two children of my own, and I try to read them a wide variety of stories. I found *Talk* in one of my son's favorite books for bedtime stories, *Favorite Folktales from Around the World* from the Pantheon Fairy Tale and Folklore Library. *Talk* is a story that always makes him giggle.

Have you dealt with the same theme in other works that you have written?

Not exactly. None of my other plays yet deal with listening as specifically as **No Talking Allowed!** does. However, I think a lot of my work generally deals with listening, or more often not listening. I'm interested in humans and how we cope with one another, and so our communication plays a large role in that. I have another work, **Let's Fix Andy**, which has a group of adult friends getting together to "fix" their hurting friend, but none of them stop long enough to actually listen to Andy's problem, which in the end is what he needs more than anything. I think everyone, including myself, could stand to listen a whole lot more.

What writers have had the most profound effect on your style?

Margaret Atwood, Sophie Treadwell, Kurt Vonnegut, Richard Brautigan, and Susan Glaspell. Growing up I read all the Vonnegut and Brautigan I could get my hands on. Their styles have a brevity and frankness I really love, and of course they all happen to be incredibly funny. I read a lot of sci-fi and fantasy now, and Margaret Atwood surprises me in the best ways, and I try, in my own writing, to think a lot about surprises and how they can bring excitement to a story. With Treadwell and Glaspell, I take their very different approaches to the everyday life, Glaspell approaching from a realistic point of view, and Treadwell using the everyday to heighten the theatricality of her work. All amazing and inspiring writers.

What do you hope to achieve with this work?

I want to give actors of all ages the chance to explore comedy and performance, and the joy of making someone laugh. I started my journey in theater as an actor, and I still haven't found something better in this world than making people laugh; it's why I write funny plays. This play also has so much physical comedy in it, something that I hope will give actors and directors a chance to explore movement and how we can connect our bodies to our voices when we're onstage.

What were the biggest challenges involved in the writing of this play?

The repetition, trying to be sure that the audience wasn't getting hit over the head again and again with the same information, since the characters have to repeat their adventure each time they meet someone new. What was tricky is that some repetition helps with the comedy, so I needed to balance that with not driving everyone crazy. What I ended up doing was printing the script and highlighting the repeating information in different colors to see how often things were said; that really helped me figure out what I needed to keep and what was getting obnoxious.

What are the most common mistakes that occur in productions of your work?

The most common mistake is when a production plays the comedy and ignores the action. Yes this play is funny, as are a lot of my other works, but all the characters have an objective, and are trying to achieve that objective each step of the way. Instead of worrying about trying to make the script funny, just concentrate on what you want, and how you're trying to get it; the comedy will take care of itself.

What inspired you to become a playwright?

I acted and directed all through high school and college, but after having my kids I didn't have the time needed for rehearsal. I'd always written—short stories, journals, boat-loads of bad poetry—so I figured I'd give writing a play a chance. Once I really dug in and concentrated on expanding my craft, I never looked back. I've found writing plays to be much more rewarding than being on the stage.

How did you research the subject?

This play didn't require much research outside of being a live human who experienced elementary and middle school, and now having small humans of my own experiencing those same things.

What is your writing process?

I always start with theme. I decide what I want to talk about with a piece before anything else. From there, I think about the situations and characters that will give me the most fertile grounds for grappling with whatever subject I intend to cover, which typically takes the longest amount of time of all my steps. Afterwards, I research (if needed), and then outline.

Writing the dialogue is the easiest and most fun part of my job, and it's always saved for almost last. Once I have a rough draft, I get actors to read it for me, make adjustments, and then repeat this step until I'm happy. Then, and finally, I send it out for production!

Shakespeare gave advice to the players in *Hamlet*; if you could give advice to your cast what would it be?
Don't just play the comedy! Go after what your character wants and the funny will come with you, I promise!

How was the first production different from the vision that you created in your mind?
I missed the first and only production of the play. It played for only two nights and I had the flu. But I heard from the director that it went over like gangbusters.

About the Author

Rachel Bublitz is an award-winning and internationally produced playwright. Her full-length play ***Cheerleaders VS. Aliens*** was commissioned and produced by the Egyptian YouTheatre in Park City, Utah. Rachel was awarded the June Anne Baker Prize from PlayGround, which honors the top female playwright in the Bay Area annually. Her play ***Ripped*** won the Detroit New Works Festival, and her ten-minute play ***Really Adult*** was a finalist for the Actors Theatre of Louisville's Heideman Award. Rachel has also worked with San Francisco Playhouse, 20% Theatre Company Chicago, Custom Made Theatre Company, Salt Lake Acting Company, the Wyoming Theater Festival, and Plan-B Theatre. She is a member of the Dramatists Guild of America and has an MA and an MFA in Creative Writing from San Francisco State University. When she isn't writing, she's chasing after her two Viking-like kids. For more, visit RachelBublitz.com.

THE LUNCH LABYRINTH
by Laura King

CAST OF CHARACTERS

PARKER, any gender, elementary school, a unique species.

FINN, any gender, elementary school, a shape-shifter.

PHOENIX, a legendary bird that can regenerate from its ashes.

SIRENS (2-10 or more), magical, mystical, musical (and kind of snooty).

KOBALOI (2-10 or more), spritely, impish, gnome-like (love to play tricks).

DRAGONS (2-10 or more), strong not-so-silent type (what with all that fire-breathing).

MINOTAURS (2-10 or more), strong, aggressive, bull-headed (literally and figuratively).

SETTING

An elementary school cafeteria.

NOTES

Sirens are beautiful but dangerous creatures whose enticing songs cause sailors to shipwreck on the rocky shores of their island.

Kobaloi are mischievous, playful creatures who love to play tricks on mortals.

Dragons are large, serpent-like creatures who breathe fire and are often used to guard treasure.

Minotaurs are creatures with the head of a bull and the body of a human who are fierce fighters but not too smart.

The Phoenix is a virtuous, solitary bird who lives for hundreds of years and is reborn from the ashes of its predecessor.

(Lights up on PARKER and FINN, who are standing outside a school cafeteria.)

PARKER: I'm not going in there!

FINN: If we don't go in, we'll starve to death!

PARKER: Please, Finn. Let's go back to the classroom.

FINN: We have to eat lunch!

PARKER: No, we don't. We could go to the playground. No one will even notice we're gone.

FINN: Parker, we're not spending the first day at our new school hiding under the jungle gym.

PARKER: But I don't want to go to the cafeteria. How will I know where to sit?

FINN: Just pick a table.

PARKER: *(Sarcastically:)* Oh, sure. Just pick a table. Just climb Mount Olympus. Just sail the River Styx.

FINN: You'll be fine.

PARKER: It's easy for you. You fit in everywhere. Why couldn't we have been identical twins? Then I could pass for you.

FINN: Come on. It'll be fine.

(Finn pulls Parker closer to the cafeteria entrance.)

PARKER: It smells funny in there.

FINN: It smells like pizza! My favorite! Let's go!

PARKER: Didn't you bring your lunch?

FINN: Yeah, but I'm not eating homemade stuff when there's pizza.

PARKER: But I packed you those cookies I made.

FINN: I can eat those anytime.

PARKER: I'm not even hungry.

FINN: You're just chicken. Oh yum, chicken. I bet they have chicken fingers in there too.

PARKER: Get your head out of your stomach!

FINN: I'm starving, so stop stalling.

PARKER: Promise you won't ditch me.

FINN: Find a place to sit and I'll get my food and find you.

(Finn starts to enter the cafeteria.)

PARKER: Wait, Finn! We can't walk right in. We have to be prepared. It's like going to a foreign land. Like Sparta or something.

FINN: You gotta stop reading all those Greek myths. Soon you'll be seeing beasts everywhere. *(Finn pulls Parker to the cafeteria entrance. Sniffing:)* Hmmm. Smell that pizza. Meet you in there.

(Finn enters the cafeteria and crosses offstage to the unseen lunch line.)

PARKER: *(Closing eyes and talking to self:)* Okay, Parker. You can do this. You just have to try to fit in.

(Lights up on the cafeteria, which contains four tables of students [a SIREN table, a KOBALOI table, a MINOTAUR table, and a DRAGON table]. Sound of a pan flute and lyre. Parker opens eyes and enters the cafeteria.)

(Determined:) The odyssey begins. *(Parker crosses to the Siren table.)* Would it be okay if I sit here?

SIREN 1: You don't look like a siren to me.

PARKER: A what?

SIREN 2: A siren, silly.

SIREN 3: The most beautiful—

SIREN 4: And most dangerous—

SIREN 5: Creatures that ever lived.

PARKER: Oh, a siren. I know what a siren is. You sing beautifully, but your songs make ships crash and sailors drown.

SIREN 6: *(Mischievously:)* Maybe we could sing something for you.

PARKER: No! I just wanted someplace to eat lunch.

SIREN 7: Sorry. This table is reserved for sirens.

SIREN 8: And you could never be a siren. I can tell by looking at you.

PARKER: I may not look like a siren, but I think I could be one if I tried hard enough.

SIREN 9: All right then. Let's hear you sing.

PARKER: Here?

SIREN 10: Go on.

> *(Parker nervously tries to sing a haunting melody. It doesn't go well. The Sirens laugh.)*

SIREN 1: You are no siren.

SIREN 2: So you can't sit with us.

SIREN 3: You would ruin our reputation.

SIREN 4: As the most—

SIREN 5: Magical—

SIREN 6: Mystical—

SIREN 7: Musical—

SIREN 8: Creatures in the cafeteria.

ALL SIRENS: So move it!

(Parker moves away as the Sirens laugh. Parker comes to the Kobaloi table.)

PARKER: Is this seat taken?

KOBALOS 1: I don't see anyone there. Do you?

KOBALOS 2: No sight of a sprite.

KOBALOS 3: No glimpse of any imps.

KOBALOS 4: Nary a fairy.

KOBALOS 5: So you're in luck, young puck.

(Kobalos 5 holds out the chair for Parker. Parker goes to sit, but Kobalos 5 pulls the chair away, causing Parker to land on the floor. The Kobaloi laugh.)

PARKER: Why did you do that?!

KOBALOS 6: Because we're kobaloi.

KOBALOS 7: We're here to annoy.

KOBALOS 8: And sometimes destroy.

KOBALOS 9: It's what we enjoy.

PARKER: Well, you know, I'm a kobalos too.

KOBALOS 10: Then do a trick.

KOBALOS 1: And make it quick.

(Parker opens lunch box, takes a napkin out, and tries to make it disappear. It doesn't go well. The Kobaloi laugh. [If possible, two of the Kobaloi can pull coins out of both of Parker's ears as they laugh.])

PARKER: Please let me stay.

KOBALOS 2: No way.

KOBALOS 3: Not today.

(The Kobaloi sit and turn their backs to Parker. Finn reenters with pizza and sits at the Dragon table.)

KOBALOS 4: *(Over shoulder:)* You brought it on yourself.

KOBALOS 5: *(Over shoulder:)* For pretending to be an elf.

KOBALOS 6: *(Over shoulder:)* Too bad you're not a goblin.

KOBALOS 7: *(Over shoulder:)* Then there wouldn't be any problem.

KOBALOS 8: You're not even a gnome.

ALL KOBALOI: Get lost. Go home.

(The Kobaloi laugh.)

FINN: Hey, Parker! Over here!

(Finn waves Parker over to the Dragon table.)

PARKER: There you are!

FINN: Meet my new friends, the dragons.

(As Parker moves closer to the table, the Dragons jump on their chairs and make fire-breathing sounds and movements. Parker is terrified.)

PARKER: Finn, we can't sit here!

FINN: Why not? They keep my pizza warm.

(Finn keeps eating pizza.)

PARKER: You don't belong here.

FINN: Sure I do. Watch.

(Finn jumps on a chair and makes fire-breathing sounds and movements. The Dragons eat pizza. As Finn returns to pizza eating, Parker rushes to the Minotaur table and sits nervously.)

MINOTAUR 1: Hey! What do you think you're doing?

PARKER: I'm sorry, but I need a place to eat lunch.

MINOTAUR 2: You can't eat here.

PARKER: There's nowhere else.

MINOTAUR 3: This table is for minotaurs only.

PARKER: I'm a minotaur.

MINOTAUR 4: Hey, everyone. This creature claims to be a minotaur.

SIREN 1: Claimed to be a siren too.

KOBALOS 1: And a kobalos.

> *(Dragons roar and snatch Finn's pizza.)*

MINOTAUR 5: Whatever you are, you're no minotaur.

MINOTAUR 6: So scram.

PARKER: *(Nervously, but defiantly:)* I'm not leaving.

MINOTAUR 7: Don't be so bull-headed.

PARKER: You're calling *me* bull-headed?

MINOTAUR 8: If the horns fit.

PARKER: Aren't you minotaurs—the most stubborn and aggressive of all creatures?

MINOTAUR 9: Don't forget strong.

MINOTAUR 10: *(Pounding fist in hand:)* Yeah.

MINOTAUR 1: So beat it or you'll learn that if you mess with the bull—

ALL MINOTAURS: You get the horns!

> *(All the creatures laugh and then go back to their lunches as an upset Parker crosses to the door.)*

FINN: Parker, come back.

(Dragons roar.)

All right, all right. Calm down.

(Finn sits back down. Parker reaches the door. Phoenix appears.)

PHOENIX: Don't run away.

PARKER: There's no place for me to sit. I don't fit it with anybody.

PHOENIX: Neither do I.

PARKER: Who are you?

PHOENIX: I'm Phoenix.

PARKER: *(Amazed:)* I've read about you. You live for centuries and then you die by the fire of the sun and are reborn from your ashes.

PHOENIX: True, but you are forgetting one important thing.

PARKER: More important than springing back to life from your burnt-up body?

PHOENIX: There is only one living phoenix in the world at one time. So, you see, I'm always alone.

PARKER: I guess we have that in common.

PHOENIX: What about your twin, Finn?

PARKER: Finn's a shape-shifter. She's/He's never alone. I tried to do that but it didn't work. Maybe I could be a phoenix like you.

PHOENIX: There is only one of me.

PARKER: Oh yeah, that's right.

PHOENIX: But there's only one of you, too. Sometimes when we shift our shapes, we lose what made us special in the first place.

(Parker turns back to look at the cafeteria creatures.)

PARKER: But I'm nothing special. Not like you or the sirens or the kobaloi or the minotaurs or even the dragons. I'm—

(Parker turns back to face Phoenix, but Phoenix is gone.)

Just me. Parker.

(Parker reenters the cafeteria and crosses by the Sirens.)

Who can't sing.

SIREN 1: Where's she/he going?

(Parker crosses by the Kobaloi.)

PARKER: Or do tricks.

KOBALOS 1: Is she/he going to sit alone?

(Parker crosses by the Dragons.)

PARKER: Or breathe fire.

(Dragon 1 roars in the form of a question. Finn tries to follow Parker, but the Dragons stop her/him. Parker crosses by the Minotaurs.)

PARKER: Or win a fight.

MINOTAUR 1: No one ever sits alone.

(Parker sees an empty table.)

PARKER: But I like to read and I know about myths and I think I'm kind of smart.

(Parker crosses to the empty table, sits, opens lunch box and removes a bag of cookies. All the creatures whisper among themselves. As Parker eats a cookie, Siren 1, Kobaloi 1 and Minotaur 1 approach Parker.)

MINOTAUR 1: So, what's the big idea?

KOBALOS 1: Who do you think you are sitting here all by yourself?

SIREN 1: Must be a chimera.

PARKER: I've got one head, not three.

KOBALOS 1: A cyclops.

PARKER: Two eyes, not one.

MINOTAUR 1: A gegenee?

PARKER: Do you see six arms?

SIREN 1: What are you then?

PARKER: Parker.

SIREN 1: A Parker? I've never heard of a Parker.

   (Finn stands.)

FINN: A Parker is a unique creature who's not afraid to be herself/himself.

   (Finn starts to cross to Parker. Dragons roar.)

Enough out of you! You're giving me a headache. I'm not going to pretend to be a dragon anymore.

   (Finn crosses to Parker's table and sits.)

PARKER: What about your pizza?

FINN: They kept burning it.

PARKER: *(Laughingly offers Finn a cookie:)* Cookie?

FINN: *(Taking the cookie:)* Thanks.

SIREN 1: Can I have one of those?

PARKER: Do sirens eat cookies?

SIREN 1: This one does!

(Siren 1 rips off costume piece to become a normal kid. Kobalos 1 and Minotaur 1 do the same.)

KOBALOS 1: I'll take one of those!

MINOTAUR 1: Me too!

(Parker distributes cookies.)

FINN: *(Taking the cookie:)* And that's another thing about Parkers. They can cook!

(Parker, Finn, Siren 1, Kobalos 1 and Minotaur 1 all eat cookies together.)

(Lights down. End of play.)

The Author Speaks

What inspired you to write this play?

When YouthPLAYS put out a call for plays for older elementary school students, I knew immediately I wanted to write a play for this collection. I have taught all age groups in my theatre teaching career, and some of my favorite students have been third through fifth graders. To me, those are the grades when reading really becomes interesting. It's also the age when students are both capable and excited about performing plays. I loved Greek mythology when I was in elementary school, so I thought it would be fun to write a play that used various creatures from Greek myths.

Was the structure or other elements of the play influenced by any other work?

The characters in *The Lunch Labyrinth* are all from Greek mythology. I tried to use a mix of familiar creatures, such as minotaurs and dragons, and lesser-known creatures, such as sirens and kobaloi. I wanted to include a phoenix in the play because I have always been fascinated by this creature and its ability to regenerate or be born again. One of my favorite characters from the *Harry Potter* series doesn't have a single line—Dumbledore's phoenix, Fawkes. The structure of this play is similar to my many other ten-minute plays published by YouthPLAYS, including plays in the collections *Lit on Fire; Bullying, Ink.; Please Say Yes; Great Expectations;* and *Youth on the Roof.*

Have you dealt with the same theme in other works that you have written?

I often write about young people who are struggling to fit in. My collection *Youth on the Roof* tells stories about teenagers trying to figure out who they are and who they want to be in the future. My play *I Know You Are But What Am I?* in the

Bullying, Ink. anthology is about teenagers confronting their own roles in the cycle of bullying. ***The Morgan Show***, which is part of the ***Great Expectations*** anthology, deals with deciding whether to conform to your parents' ideas about you or stand firm in who you are. ***Ante Up***, in the ***Please Say Yes*** anthology, is about two young people who decide to finally give up playing it cool. I love exploring how young people find their way in the world with all the pressures that they have to deal with: social, parental and personal.

What writers have had the most profound effect on your style?

I love reading plays by other playwrights who write for young people. Some of my favorite YouthPLAYS writers include Nicole B. Adkins, Matt Buchanan, Jonathan Dorf, Claudia Haas and Randy Wyatt. I recently read ***Kid Turboni Brings the Rain*** by Mark J. Costello, winner of the 2018 American Alliance for Theatre & Education (AATE) Distinguished Play Award, and loved it. I'm also influenced by plays written by young playwrights. I think the best way to learn how to write for younger audiences is to read plays written by younger playwrights.

What do you hope to achieve with this work?

On one level, I want to introduce elementary students to some of the creatures found in Greek myths. I hope to pique their interest in Greek mythology and inspire them to learn more about this type of literature. On another level, I want young people to realize that everyone is afraid of new experiences and fitting in. The most important thing is that you remain true to yourself. In one way or another, we are all phoenixes.

What are the most common mistakes that occur in productions of your work?

I don't like to think in terms of mistakes but rather opportunities. Even when I see one of my plays produced in a way that I wouldn't have chosen, I always learn something from the experience. I think actors are one of the greatest resources for playwrights. Watching what an actor brings to a character (even if at first it seems like a mistake) always informs my writing. Why did the actor make that choice? Is there something in the play that led the actor to this choice? If I'm watching a production that doesn't seem to align with my original idea of the play, I ask myself why the director went in this direction. Sometimes these questions lead me in a whole new direction and end up improving the play.

What inspired you to become a playwright?
From sixth grade on, I was always involved in theatre. I've been writing plays for about eight years. I used to act but stopped when I wanted to raise my daughter. When she was older, I thought I would return; however, because we had moved to a less populated area, it was difficult for me to travel to more urban areas, where the majority of theaters are. As I was struggling with how to stay involved in this field that I loved, I took a playwriting class. From that moment on, I knew that I wanted to write plays. I decided that to do it well, I needed more education, so I enrolled in the MFA in playwriting program at Hollins University. I graduated in 2016 and have been writing, studying and teaching playwriting ever since.

How did you research the subject?
I did a lot of internet research on Greek mythology. It had been a while since I had read any Greek myths. I had fun reencountering some of the mythical creatures I used to read about in my youth. I even came across several creatures I had never learned about, for example, the kobaloi. I was looking for a classic trickster character. I knew about Hermes and Loki, but I wanted a group of tricksters, not just one specific person. That's when I discovered the kobaloi, who are sprites that like

to trick and frighten mortals. Parents even used tales of the kobaloi to frighten children into behaving.

Are any characters modeled after real life or historical figures?

All the characters are modeled on creatures from Greek mythology. The Sirens are based on the sirens from Homer's *The Odyssey*—those beautiful but dangerous creatures that Odysseus longed to hear sing. The Kobaloi represent all those mischievous creatures who love to play tricks on mortals. The Dragons were inspired by the dragons in *Harry Potter and the Goblet of Fire* by J. K. Rowling. I wanted to find a particularly stubborn creature, and that's when I remembered the Minotaurs, who have the head of a bull and the body of a human (hence, bull-headed!). Finally, I had to include my favorite creature—the exotic, mysterious and solitary Phoenix.

What is your writing process?

I try to write my first draft without censoring myself. I write whatever pops into my mind, even if it's crazy! I like to see where my mind takes me. After I have completed the first draft, I think for a long time about what the play is really about—what do I want to say with this play? Then I complete a second draft with that question in mind. After that, I need to hear the play read aloud, so I try to have a formal reading or at least have some friends or students read it aloud. Then I revise again. I often ask myself, "Are plays ever really finished?" I think the answer is no.

Shakespeare gave advice to the players in *Hamlet*; if you could give advice to your cast what would it be?

My best advice is to be prepared and then relax and have fun. The relax and have fun part is only possible if you are prepared. There is a reason we rehearse plays. If you put in the hard work, you are usually rewarded when the show opens.

About the Author

Laura King is an award-winning playwright and instructor of theatre at Gordon State College in Georgia. She holds an MFA in playwriting from Hollins University and is a member of the Dramatists Guild, the Southeastern Theatre Conference and Working Title Playwrights. Along with her YouthPLAYS plays, her work is available at Stage Rights, Polychoron Press and the New Play Exchange. For more information, please visit laurakingplaywright.com.

THE CATNAPPER MYSTERY
by Isabella Russell-Ides

CAST OF CHARACTERS

TWILA JAMES, a suspected witch, female.

TULIP HOPKINS, a nosey neighbor, female.

BRAT, a cat, either, who later is revealed to be Blake/Blaze.

JAKE/JANET, a catnapper, either, and sibling of Blake/Blaze.

OFFICER SIEBEL, a detective, either.

SIGNS, three players indicating scene changes (optional), either.

While Jake/Janet and Blake/Blaze use male pronouns/nouns in the body of the script, if your production uses females instead, just use female names and the corresponding pronouns/nouns (e.g. she instead of he, sister instead of brother).

SETTING

Scene 1: Twila James' Garden.

Scene 2: Tulip Hopkins' Parlor.

Scene 3: Jake's Cabin.

SCENE 1: Twila James' Garden

(SIGN #1, an actor with a flowerpot hat, enters. TWILA, on her hands and knees furiously pulls weeds. BRAT the cat naps in the shade. TULIP stands behind her hand-held window frame, pulling curtain aside occasionally to spy.)

TWILA: Weeds. Weeds. Weeds. This is all your fault, you know.

BRAT: Meow.

(CATNAPPER JAKE/JANET enters, holding fake tree to hide behind. Jake wears sunglasses.)

TWILA: Haven't you got anything better to say for yourself, Mr. Brat the cat?

BRAT: Meow.

TWILA: OH Meeeeooooow to you. You and your one-word vocabulary are driving me nuts! And this heat. I need a break, thank you very much, Mr. made-in-the-shade. I'm going to get some lemonade.

(Tulip pokes her head out through her fake window.)

And THANK YOU, Tulip Hopkins, for minding your own business!

(Twila exits. Tulip quickly pulls curtain shut and reopens after Twila exits.)

JAKE: *(Jumping out from hiding place:)* Coast is clear.

BRAT: *(Arching his back, hissing:)* MEEEOOOOOOOOW!!

JAKE: Shhhh. *(Slowly approaching:)* Nice kitty. Nice kitty.

BRAT: Meow.

JAKE: Here, I've got a treat for you. Don't be a scaredy-cat.

(Places an open can of tuna on the floor. As Brat eats, Jake puts leash around Brat's neck.)

Nice kitty. Good kitty. Okay, cat, I don't know how to tell you this but we've got to get out of here and I mean fast!

BRAT: Meow? Meow.

JAKE: YES. Yes. It's me!

BRAT: Meow?

JAKE: Hey, would I lie to you? C'mon. Let's go!

(Jake exits with Brat on leash. Twila enters, cell phone in her pocket.)

TWILA: Brat! Oh Brat! The cat is missing. Oh, no. Now what! This is mighty suspicious, if you ask me. Brat never leaves the shade. That is one spoiled, lazy cat.

TULIP: *(Parting curtain:)* Are you talking to yourself, Twila?

TWILA: Yes, Tulip, I am.

TULIP: Do you mind if I say something?

TWILA: Yes, of course I mind. It's a private conversation, thank you very much.

TULIP: Suit yourself.

(Tulip closes curtain. Twila takes out cell, dials 9-1-1.)

TWILA: Nine. One. One. Hello. Hello. This is an emergency. Someone just catnapped the kid, no I mean kidnapped the cat. No. Yes. What I'm trying to say is that my cat is a missing person. No, I don't mean that. Just get here as fast as you can. Please. *(Pacing back and forth:)* My name is Twila James. I live at six, zero, zero, zero Witchy Way. Hurry. Please. This is my most desperate hour.

(A police siren is heard, Twila paces. OFFICER SIEBEL enters, with briefcase and detective paraphernalia.)

OFFICER SIEBEL: Hello Ma'am. Police Officer, Detective Siebel.

TWILA: That was fast.

SIEBEL: I was in the 'hood when the report came over the radio. Speed is everything. Either you find them in the first twenty-four hours or the missing stay missing.

TWILA: *(Pacing:)* Oh, dear. Oh, dear. Oh, dear. That poor cat.

SIEBEL: Did you say cat?

TWILA: Yes, Brat, the cat. Here's a picture. We could post it online. He was right here. Seconds ago. Right here. In the shade.

SIEBEL: Ma'am! Please. Control yourself. You are trampling all over the crime scene.

TWILA: Sorry, Officer.

SIEBEL: *(With magnifying glass, on hands and knees:)* There are valuable clues right here underfoot. Please move your foot. Pick it up. Pick it up.

TWILA: My foot?

SIEBEL: Yes.

(Twila picks up her foot, stands on one leg.)

SEIBEL: Ah HA! A clue. This case will be made in the shade.

TWILA: May I put my foot down?

SIEBEL: Yes, but be careful where you put it down. No! Not there.

TWILA: Here?

SIEBEL: Yes. Look here. Prints. You see how the cat prints go off in that direction.

TWILA: You're a genius.

SIEBEL: Yes, I am. There are two sets of prints. Cat prints and human footprints going off in the same direction. And look here! *(Slipping on surgical gloves:)* What is this?

TWILA: It's a tuna can.

SIEBEL: My thoughts exactly! Please hold the evidence bag.

   (Places tuna can in baggie.)

TWILA: I can explain the tuna can.

SIEBEL: No, please. This is a most intriguing case. Allow me to review. We have two clues. Footprints and a tuna can! And now I must ask you, did you see anyone suspicious in the neighborhood?

TWILA: Well, yes. It was odd. It was hot. I was pulling weeds. But out of the corner of my eye, I thought I saw someone dart behind a tree. And now the tree is missing!

   (Siebel takes out sketchpad, begins to draw.)

SIEBEL: Excellent observation. Details. Details. Give me more details. Concentrate.

TWILA: It's coming back. It was a boy, holding a tree.

SIEBEL: Ah HAH. The old hide-behind-the-cardboard-tree trick. A classic. I need more. Close your eyes. Concentrate.

TWILA: *(Closing eyes:)* Yes. Yes. I can see him, plain as daylight. He was wearing big black sunglasses.

SIEBEL: Ah HA! Shades! This case will be made in the shade, just like I said. Here, look at this.

   (SIEBEL shows Twila a drawing.)

TWILA: Amazing. That's him! You *are* a genius.

SIEBEL: Speed is my watchword. Now, is there anyone else you can think of who might provide valuable clues for my investigation?

TWILA: I suppose you could interview my nosey neighbor, Tulip Hopkins.

(Twila points to Tulip, who promptly closes her curtain on her hand-held fake window.)

SIEBEL: Excellent idea. Good day, ma'am.

TWILA: Thank you, officer. Good day and good luck.

(Twila exits.)

SCENE 2: Tulip's Parlor

(SIGN #2, an actor with a teapot hat, enters. Siebel goes "next door," knocks on Tulip's door.)

SIEBEL: Knock. Knock.

TULIP: *(Putting down "window":)* Who's there?

SIEBEL: Officer Siebel.

TULIP: Officer Siebel who?

SIEBEL: Officer Siebel, First Detective, Forty-Third Precinct.

TULIP: My turn. Knock. Knock.

SIEBEL: Who's there?

TULIP: Tulip.

SIEBEL: Tulip who?

TULIP: Two lips for you to kiss.

SIEBEL: Please, Ma'am. This is official police business. I've got no time for monkey business.

TULIP: You're no fun.

SIEBEL: We better start over. Knock. Knock.

TULIP: Who's there?

SIEBEL: Canoe.

TULIP: Canoe who?

SIEBEL: Canoe answer a few simple questions, Ma'am?

TULIP: Be glad to. Please come in. Take a seat.

SIEBEL: I was wondering if you noticed anything suspicious around the neighborhood in the last 48 hours?

TULIP: I certainly have! Well. There was this darling boy who used to help Twila James in her garden. Pulling weeds and stuff like that. Well. Yesterday, I heard Twila yelling at him, calling him a brat. AND things much more terrible than that. Just because that poor boy ate some strawberries from her precious strawberry patch. Shocking. It was just shocking.

SIEBEL: I'm sure it was, Ma'am. But I am not interested in gossip. Just the facts, Ma'am. This is a scientific investigation and I am looking for clues as to the disappearance of your neighbor's cat.

TULIP: That's just what I'm trying to tell you. After the big argument, that darling boy was never seen again! AND. That very afternoon the cat showed up. See what I'm saying? Boy disappears. Cat shows up. Fact one and fact two.

SIEBEL: Very interesting. BUT. Is it a coincidence or is there a connection? That is the question. *(Taking out the drawing of the suspect:)* Here. Take a look at this. This is our prime suspect. Do you recognize him?

TULIP: Why, yes! Yes. If you take away the sunglasses, I'm sure I've seen a boy who looks just like that hanging around the neighborhood. I bet he's one of the kids from the summer camp down by the lake. Just follow that road until you get to the lake, you'll see the cabins on the left.

SIEBEL: Thank you, Ma'am. I'll be off, then. You've been most helpful.

(Siebel exits.)

TULIP: My pleasure, Officer. I'm sure.

SCENE 3: Jake's Cabin at the Lake

(SIGN #3, an actor with a Lincoln Log hat, enters.)

JAKE: *(To Brat:)* Gosh, this is a fine mess you've gotten us into. What am I going to tell Mom?

BRAT: Meow.

JAKE: Right. I go off to summer camp and Mom says, "Promise me, you'll watch out for your little brother." Now what am I supposed to say? Gee Mom, I'm really sorry but someone turned Blake into a cat. I'm going to be in so much trouble!

SIEBEL: *(At cabin "door":)* Knock. Knock.

JAKE: Who's there?

SIEBEL: Police.

JAKE: Police who?

SIEBEL: Police come out and answer a few questions.

JAKE: *(To Brat:)* Did you hear that? It's the police. What should I do?

SIEBEL: Knock. Knock.

JAKE: Just a minute! Brat, I mean Blake, you've got to hide. Here. Hold this.

(Cat holds the cardboard tree from earlier scene.)

SIEBEL: *(Louder:)* I said knock, knock.

JAKE: Yeah. Um. Come in. I guess.

SIEBEL: *(Entering:)* Police officer, Detective Siebel. *(Showing badge:)* And you are?

JAKE: Who me? I'm nobody. I'm just an innocent bystander.

SIEBEL: Do you have a name, Mister Innocent Bystander?

JAKE: Yes, I have a name. But so what? I don't know anything about any cat burglars.

SIEBEL: Ah HA! No one mentioned anything about cat burglars. Very suspicious. Things will go a lot smoother if you co-operate. I understand from the camp counselor that you have a brother who shares this cabin with you.

JAKE: A brother? Yeah. Sure. I have one of those.

BRAT: Meow.

SIEBEL: What was that?

JAKE: Nothing. It was nothing.

SIEBEL: Where is your brother?

BRAT: *(Entering:)* MEEeeeeooooWW!!

JAKE: I don't know how say this but, that's my brother. His name is Blake.

SIEBEL: I don't know how to say this Jake, but that's a cat. In fact, it looks exactly like the cat in the photo Twila James gave me. The very cat that was snatched from her front yard at six, zero, zero, zero Witchy Way. Do you by any chance own a pair of black sunglasses?

JAKE: Um, yes. They're right here. It's not against the law to own sunglasses.

SIEBEL: Would you please put them on?

> *(Jake does.)*

Ah HA! Would you by any chance own a fake tree?

JAKE: It's not against the law to own a fake tree.

SIEBEL: Would you mind standing behind the fake tree?

JAKE: Okay. I guess.

TULIP: *(At cabin "door":)* Knock. Knock.

JAKE: Who's there?

TULIP: Tulip.

SIEBEL: Don't say it!

JAKE: Say what?

SIEBEL: Tulip who?

TULIP: Two lips for you to kiss. *(Entering:)* Oh my! Oh, lordy, lordy. It's him. The boy in the composite police drawing.

TWILA: Knock. Knock.

SIEBEL: Who's there?

TWILA: Twila James. *(Entering "cabin":)* Tulip Hopkins! What are you doing here?

TULIP: I came here to make sure that you do the right thing, Twila James!

TWILA: It's none of your business, you old snoop!

SIEBEL: Ladies. Ladies please! Miss Twila James, is that your missing cat?

JAKE: No! It's not her cat. It's my brother.

TULIP: The boy is right. Twila turned his brother into a cat.

TWILA: Tulip!

TULIP: I didn't see her do it. But I know she did it because she's a witch!

TWILA: It takes one to know one, Tulip Hopkins.

TULIP: I admit it. I am a witch. And proud of it. *(Taking out hankie and starting to cry loudly:)* And I used to be proud of Twila. She was such a good witch. It's hard to believe she would do something so unforgivably cruel.

TWILA: It was an accident, Tulip! My word, we've known each other for hundreds of years. Do you think I'd do something like that on purpose? He ate my strawberries. I lost my temper. I called him a brat. It rhymes with cat. The spell was cast. And that was that. It takes 24 hours to reverse an accidental curse. ShaZAMMM!!

BLAKE: *(Removing cat ears or mask:)* Hey, everybody, I'm me again.

JAKE: Blake!

BLAKE: Wow. That was awesome.

SIEBEL: Blake/Blaine, do you want to press charges?

BLAKE: No way. That was the greatest adventure of my life. I'll be famous. The boy who was a cat for 24 hours.

JAKE: Yeah, but no one will ever believe it. I saw it and I don't believe it.

BLAKE: Aw, shoot. Oh well, it doesn't matter, does it? Because we'll always remember. Right, Bro/Sis? You rescued me! You're the best brother/sister ever! And thanks for the tuna, Jake. It was pretty tasty. But next time add a little mayo.

JAKE: Really Blake? Add mayo?

BLAKE: Meow.

(Jake puts hands on hips, gives Blake the screw-eye.)

Just kidding.

TULIP: Aren't they just the best? Brothers and best friends forever.

TWILA: We used to be best friends forever.

TULIP: Want to get the brooms out like the old days?

TWILA: Yes! Let's play tag the moon.

(Twila and Tulip exit.)

SIEBEL: Looks like everything turned out just fine. I solved the Catnapper Mystery. The witches made friends. Jake's brother Blake is no longer a cat.

JAKE: *(To Blake:)* Hey, what's that?

(Blake turns around; he has a cat tail.)

BLAKE: What is it? *(Holding tail:)* Oh, no.

SIEBEL: A cat tail!

(Blows police whistle.)

Stop. Witches.

JAKE: Come on!

(All exit running, this can include the "Signs." If staged in classroom, actors can run around periphery. Optional Keystone Cops music. All exit.)

(Offstage, Officer Siebel blows police whistle. End of play.)

The Author Speaks

What inspired you to write this play?

The children who played the original roles were my inspiration. I asked my group of young actors what parts they wanted to play before I wrote the play. One girl, whose father was a police officer, wanted to be a detective. Two girls wanted to be witches. One boy wanted to be a cat. And one boy wanted to be "just a boy."

Was the structure or other elements of the play influenced by any other work?

No, not really. The children made suggestions about what they wanted to say or do. I felt like a fairy godmother granting wishes. The boy who played the cat was shy and only wanted to meow. It was a lot of fun trying to make his meowing matter.

Have you dealt with the same theme in other works that you have written?

I have a pair of sisters in one of my adult plays, **Leonard's Car**, who move from resentment to renewal, just as the former friends Twila and Tulip do in **The Catnapper Mystery**. I never thought of that until just this minute. In my full-length play, **The Secret Garden**, Mary Lennox has a temper that must be tamed. Twila's temper in **The Catnapper Mystery** drives the precipitating action, and in the play's resolution, Twila must make amends.

What writers have had the most profound effect on your style?

With the plays that I write for young children, I try to get as close as I can to the way children talk to each other. So even though in this play, the two witches are "adults," they speak kidspeak. This play was based on improvisations and truly grew from the children.

What do you hope to achieve with this work?
This work is meant to let children experience the joy of performance. It is fun and funny. The lines are easy to memorize, minimizing performance anxiety. The children can make their own costumes. The walk-on players can make their own signs. It is designed to be a play young players can own. It doesn't need a stage. The play works well in a classroom.

What were the biggest challenges involved in the writing of this play?
One interesting challenge was the construction of the window that the nosy neighbor Tulip Hawkins looks out from. We chose a hand-held window made of foam-core board, with a moveable curtain.

What inspired you to become a playwright?
I fell in love with a musician who needed someone to write a libretto for his country western musical, ***Nashville Road***. The show was fabulous and fun, so I fell in love with theatre. I am still married to the musician and still writing for theatre.

Shakespeare gave advice to the players in Hamlet; if you could give advice to your cast what would it be?
Imagine that you are talking to your character. Ask your character if there is something special they would like to wear in the play, something you can add to the costume. Go find it, or make it, or borrow it. It's a nice way to make friends with your character.

About the Author

Isabella Russell-Ides grew up under the Hollywood sign. Her father ran searchlights for the openings of red-carpet premieres, so she was leaning towards the stage lights from the get go. Her two adaptions for YouthPLAYS, ***Little Women*** and ***The Secret Garden***, were labors of love, designed to give a fresh feel to these beloved classics. ***The Catnapper Mystery*** was written as a classroom play when she worked as an elementary creative consultant. Her critically acclaimed plays have seen productions across the US. ***The Early Education of Conrad Eppler*** won Echo Theatre's national Big Shout Out competition and is now a novel: *White Monkey Chronicles: The Complete Trilogy*. ***CoCo & Gigi*** (a Beckett-inspired parlay) and ***Lydie Marland in the Afterlife*** premiered to showers of critical praise. ***Leonard's Car*** won Nora's Playhouse Outstanding New Play award in NYC. Her plays have garnered Leon Rabin Awards, The Column Awards, Critics Forum Awards, Best Of Fest accolades. Russell-Ides is also a published poet.

THE SILENT ONES
by Catherine Castellani

CAST OF CHARACTERS

LETTER K, a consonant with a chip on their shoulder.

LETTER W, a happy consonant.

LETTER L, a dreamy consonant.

LETTER B, a pompous consonant.

LETTER C, a feline consonant, changeable and tricky.

Consonants may be played by performers of any gender. Feel free to update pronouns in dialogue to reflect your casting.

SETTING

The hideout of the newly formed Secret Society of Silent Consonants is a basement with properly "underground" qualities such as bars on the covered windows, exposed brick, and ratty, mismatched furniture. The door has a speakeasy window that can be pulled open and shut.

PRODUCTION NOTES

Each letter wears their letter somehow on their costume: a cape covered in Bs, a jeweled medallion W, etc. Ideally, costumes are something out of *The Three Musketeers* trunk: frilly tops, capes, hats, knickers on K for a visual pun. But a simple felt letter will do.

ACKNOWLEDGMENT

The original production of **The Silent Ones** was done by Turtle Shell Productions as part of their 8-Minute Madness Festival.

Artistic Director/Producer: John W. Cooper, Times Square Theatre, New York City, January 21—February 5, 2011. Directed by Mikaela Kafka with the following cast:

LETTER K...Christina Hanos
LETTER W...Megan Doyle
LETTER L...Lydia Batten
LETTER B...Janaries Velasquez
LETTER C...Brielee Lu

DEDICATION

Inspired by and dedicated to The Resident Child, Angelica Hori, whose spelling homework was unexpectedly dramatic.

(There is a round wooden table with four mismatched chairs center stage, perhaps a candle flickering on it. Smaller tables may flank it to the left and right, but give the main table plenty of room.)

(LETTER K is seated at the main table, brooding. There is a sound of howling wind and a clap of thunder. Then a knock at the door. K ignores it. Another knock. W enters from stage right and confronts K.)

W: Someone is knocking!

K: I can hear that, W.

W: K! Knocking! K-N-O-C-K-I-N-G. Shouldn't you answer? You're a silent K!

K: Me, answer? A-N-S-W-E-R. You're a silent W. You answer it.

(W goes to the door and slides open the window cover.)

W: Who goes there?

L: It is L.

K: L? She's not silent!

W: Quiet! You be silent! I'm doing this! What is your password, L?

L: Walk. W-A-L-K. That's a silent L.

W: Oh walk! And it starts with a W!

(W opens the door joyfully. L enters, holding an elaborate mask on a stick before their face to shield their identity.)

K: And ends with a K. Yes, W. You get so enthusiastic about regular consonants. May I remind you that this is a *secret* society of *silent* consonants? Only those letters that appear silently in the English language may join.

L: Then I am in the right place. At last. At last I can be myself.

(With great relief, L sinks into a chair and discards the mask.)

W: How did you hear about us? How did you find us?

L: It was just a whisper. From H. In an herb garden. He was wandering about the lavender, and I asked him what he was doing there. He said, "can't you spell herb?" Of course I can! But seeing H, for a moment I forgot: H-E-R-B. And then he told me, just hinted, that there were others. Perfectly normal consonants by day with an entirely silent and secret identity by night. I had to find you.

K: I couldn't stand it, always being identified as the hard, aggressive "K" sound, when I know how sneaky I can be! It was like a knife in the gut every time I appeared in a children's book. Every time! Kangaroo! Never knuckle!

L: How many of us are there?

K: Few.

W: Well…

K: There can't be many, W.

W: D was very interested.

K: D?

W: Fudge, bridge, fridge. I told him I could hear a D in there. Don't you? It's not good enough to pass in some accents. It's got to be a regular thing, silent all the time.

L: In bridge I hear it. But fudge? Wait, what about Wednesday? D could have a case!

K: I'll decide that!

W: The club is his idea. K is touchy about it.

K: Secret society! Not a club. A secret society of silent consonants. Where's the secret, where's the mystery, where's the exclusivity, if all 21 consonants can up and join?

L: What if they have a password?

K: I'll decide that! And fudge is not going to cut it, not with me! D is not silent.

> *(Clap of thunder, howl of wind. K is sulking. There is a mighty knock on the door.)*

I will handle this.

> *(K stalks to the door and pulls open the speakeasy window.)*

Who goes there?

B: It is B. Let me in. I am a silent consonant seeking fellows.

W: What?

L: B is so pompous. First consonant and all.

W: Oh so what!

K: I doubt very much that you're a silent consonant, B. Go away.

B: You doubt me?

K: I do.

B: I said, you *doubt* me?

K: I—wait!

B: D-O-U-B-T. Utterly silent. Now open this door. The wind is frightful.

> *(K opens the door and B sweeps into the room, swirling a great cape with a flourish, and striking a pose. B is wearing a black "Lone Ranger" type mask.)*

I was told there would be cocoa.

W: Yeah, yeah. I'll get it.

> *(W exits.)*

B: This is quite a small gathering.

K: It's a secret society, B.

B: Well I expect we'll be joined by G and H any time now. And there are bound to be others. Wait until they get their dictionaries out.

> (*W returns with a tray and four mismatched cups and mugs of cocoa.*)

L: Thank you, W!

> (*They all sit to enjoy cocoa. There is a slow, insistent knock on the door.*)

K: Don't answer it.

> (*The mysterious knock is repeated.*)

L: Why?

K: I have a bad feeling about this...

B: Nonsense.

> (*B stalks to the door, dramatically sweeps the cape back, and opens the speakeasy window.*)

K: B, sit down!

B: Who goes there?

C: Open the door. It is C, a most changeable letter, and indisputably silent at times.

K: NO NO NO!

B: Password?

C: Muscle.

K: Muscle?

W: She's right. That's a silent C: M-U-S-C-L-E.

L: That's right. We're right next to each other, and you never hear her.

K: Oh please, not C. She's the bane of my existence.

(B throws the door open. C, wearing a long cape with a large hood that hides their face, enters very slowly and then slowly lowers the mask.)

C: Cocoa. Two Cs. Perfect.

W: I'll get you a cup.

K: No. Get her a mug. Nothing with C, please.

C: If I'd known you were here, K —

K: Oh you knew all right! You're stalking me!

C: We're thrown together so often. Fate…

K: Shut up! [Stop talking!]

B: Rudeness! C is certainly silent in muscle!

C: And scissors. And czar. Though T also claims tsar, in the T-S-A-R alternate spelling.

K: T? We're going to have T in here!?

(W returns with a delicate cup of cocoa.)

W: Sounds like T qualifies.

K: Ruined! My plan, my dream! All ruined.

(L, W, and B enjoy their cocoa. K stalks downstage to avoid them all. C follows.)

C: You knew very well I'd be here.

K: I suppose I should have thought it through. Yes. You find a way into everything.

C: Why don't you just admit you enjoy my company and drop the antagonism? You don't fool anybody.

K: I don't enjoy your company! I prefer to work alone! Don't you see? A secret society is about standing apart. It's about stepping away from the herd.

C: And banding together with your fellows.

L: It's not a society if there is only one member, K.

W: Admit it. You were lonely.

B: I say, K, your cocoa will get cold. Join us!

(C returns to the table, reluctantly joined by K. There are only four chairs, so K stands to drink their cocoa. K raises a mug to them all.)

K: To the Silent Consonants of the English Language!

ALL: Bravo!

(They sip. There is a knock at the door. All turn and look.)

(Blackout. End of play.)

The Author Speaks

What inspired you to write this play?
When my daughter was in first grade, one of her teachers was dead-set against learning to spell. (There was an educational theory involved, but I refuse to entertain it here.) I come from a school that was in love with spelling bees. It was a bit of a conflict. Second grade was a whole other world—lots of fantastic spelling homework! My daughter would talk about letters as if they were people who were up to mysterious business, showing up silent here and loud there. So I wrote her a series of plays. She couldn't have been more thrilled than when we went to see "her" plays in the theater.

Was the structure or other elements of the play influenced by any other work?
Not consciously or specifically. But a secret fort or club is a staple of children's literature, so I'm sure that's seeped into my creative outlook.

Have you dealt with the same theme in other works that you have written?
Yes! *There Is No E in Ski* was produced along with *The Silent Ones*. And since then I've written a few more spelling plays in a set I call *Alphabet City*. For years I lived in New York City's East Village, which is also called Alphabet City because when you go east of First Avenue you hit Avenue A, B, C and D. The other plays are *The Occasionals*, about a gang of little-used consonants, and *H is for Halloween* about the mysterious powers of H.

What writers have had the most profound effect on your style?
I have studied a lot with playwright Rogelio Martinez, and his attention to structure has been very important to my development as a writer. His play *Ping Pong* is a good

example of how to mix research, humor, history, and the telling detail. I'm a big fan of David Ives' short plays, and I know they've had a big effect on how I approach short work. I especially like his short play **The Philadelphia**. Another structure king is Michael Frayn, author of **Noises Off** and **Copenhagen**, a farce and a historical drama. It's my goal to develop that kind of range!

What do you hope to achieve with this work?
I love the English language, absurd spelling conventions and all. I'd love it if kids got a kick out of the play and started to notice spelling as something fun and revealing, not just a chore. English is a huge language, with more words in active use than any other language currently spoken on earth! I love looking up the etymology of unfamiliar words, or discovering that a spelling or usage was invented by Shakespeare, or is an Anglicized approximation of a word in Chinese or Hungarian. I'm a word nerd. I'm passing it on.

What were the biggest challenges involved in the writing of this play?
None of the consonants has a gender. They're letters of the alphabet! I want the play to be available to anyone who wants to perform. But I did find that I would slip into writing he or she instead of it.

What are the most common mistakes that occur in productions of your work?
Actors like to reshape the language to be easier, but that flattens out the rhythm of the play. For example, Letter K is tremendously ambitious and full of itself, B is pompous, C is sinuous and sneaky. Making their language more "natural" by fudging the lines erases what's fun and different about their characters, what makes them unique. So learn your lines, kids. Precisely.

What inspired you to become a playwright?
I did a lot of theatre when I was a kid, mostly musicals staged at my schools and community theatres. I thought I was going to be an actress! Then I moved to New York and went to acting school. My classmates were really, really good. Much better than I. It was a golden opportunity to learn to write and stage theatre with a room full of really fine performers who needed opportunities to shine. It was a lot more fun dreaming up roles for my friends than ineptly performing.

How did you research the subject?
The Silent Ones draws on a lifetime of spelling, but I did try to give each letter lots of opportunities to use their own words. At the time I wrote it, my daughter was just learning about silent consonants, so I definitely used her interests and questions as a guide.

What is your writing process?
Sit down. Start. Keep going. Finish. Get a bunch of actor friends together to read it out loud. Rewrite it. It can get sticky at any point along the way but that's the basic job description.

Shakespeare gave advice to the players in *Hamlet*; if you could give advice to your cast what would it be?
Release your inner ham, your outer ham, and if you're not a ham, pretend you're a ham. While Shakespeare demands truly fine acting by classically trained performers, *The Silent Ones* is best with shameless overacting, enormous gesture, and histrionics. Oh, and learn your lines. Precisely. (And trust the director. The director will tell you if you're really too ridiculous.)

How was the first production different from the vision that you created in your mind?
I had pictured all the letters the same age, as in a classroom. The original cast ranged from age 8 to age 15! It was a really

fun and surprising mix of energies.

About the Author

Catherine Castellani's plays include *The Red Flags, 2Y20M, The Bigsley Project, In Search of Lost Time, The Mongoose and the Cobra,* and *Possession* (finalist for the Marion International Fellowship). Her short plays *Work, Gestation,* and *Organization Man* were Heideman Award finalists. Short works for young spellers include *There Is No E in Ski* and *The Silent Ones*, both produced by 8-Minute Madness Festival. Catherine has twice been a resident at the MacDowell Colony and is a one-time resident at the Ucross Foundation. She studied at NYU's Tisch School of the Arts Experimental Theater Wing (New York and Paris programs) and is a member of The Dramatists Guild.

HOW BLUE IS MY CROCODILE
by Arthur M. Jolly

CAST OF CHARACTERS

MADISON, 11 years old, full of ideas and suggestions, she is suppressing her fears.

RACHEL, 9 years old, creative and amenable, she is unaware of her fears.

SETTING

A kitchen. A table and chair, practical.

While mentioned, the rug and fridge are imaginary.

TIME

The present.

PRODUCTION HISTORY

The play received a staged reading in Austin, Texas, March 2009, and premiered in Los Angeles, June 2009 with Renée Gauthier as Madison, and Andrea Gauthier as Rachel, directed by Danielle Ozymandias.

(MADISON sits on a chair, as RACHEL looks out a window.)

MADISON: D'you see them?

RACHEL: Not yet. There's a crocodile.

MADISON: Don't be silly.

RACHEL: There is! It's bright red and as big as the whole street.

MADISON: That's not a crocodile. That's an alligator.

RACHEL: Are you sure?

MADISON: Yup. Crocodiles are blue.

RACHEL: Actually, I think it's a fire truck.

MADISON: That's just stupid.

RACHEL: There's a fireman wearing a yellow helmet driving it.

MADISON: Firemen never wear helmets when they drive—they put them on when they get there; so it must be an alligator.

RACHEL: Then I guess the fireman's driving a big red alligator.

MADISON: See? I'm always right.

RACHEL: It has shiny wheels.

MADISON: But it's not them?

RACHEL: No. I don't think he'll come home on an alligator.

MADISON: Should we get it ready?

RACHEL: Alligators are always ready. Crocodiles are late.

MADISON: I was talking about the cake.

RACHEL: The cake?

MADISON: The cake.

RACHEL: What cake?

MADISON: There's only one cake.

RACHEL: For everyone? Everyone in the whole world?

RACHEL: One cake for all.

RACHEL: For daddy. For coming home.

MADISON: Most of him.

RACHEL: Except a toe. Who's gonna miss a toe?

MADISON: She didn't say toe, she said foot.

RACHEL: Part of a foot. Mom said part of his foot. Part of his foot is a toe.

MADISON: If it was a toe, he wouldn't be in a wheelchair.

RACHEL: It's only for a while.

MADISON: Til he gets better.

RACHEL: It will get better?

MADISON: Til he learns to walk without it.

RACHEL: He told me he wasn't going to be in a wheelchair. He said he would come home riding a big red crocodile.

MADISON: Crocodiles are —

RACHEL: I know. He was going to get a blue one and paint it.

MADISON: Paint it.

RACHEL: And put twirly lights on the top and big shiny wheels and a siren.

MADISON: Would he wear a helmet?

RACHEL: The crocodile?

MADISON: Daddy.

RACHEL: He would wear three helmets! One on his head, and one on each foot so that he could come home with all his toes.

MADISON: And we'd make him a big cake.

RACHEL: The biggest cake in the whole world.

MADISON: And we'd write "welcome hom" on it.

RACHEL: Hom?

MADISON: I ran out of room for the "E".

RACHEL: Then it's not the biggest cake in the world.

MADISON: It was the biggest pan we had. And it is too the biggest cake in the world, it's as big as Michigan. The E fell into lake Erie and got lost, is all. The letters are so big, you can only see them from up in the air.

RACHEL: In his helicopter.

MADISON: When he comes in the door, we hold out the cake and we say "Eeee".

RACHEL: Eeee?

MADISON: Eeeeeeeeee.

RACHEL: I'm gonna say "welcome home, Daddy" and I'm gonna jump up in his arms, and he'll spin me around and around like a helicopter.

MADISON: No, he won't.

RACHEL: Yes he will.

MADISON: He's in a wheelchair.

(Rachel stops dead.)

Mom will have to help him up the new ramp, and then he'll have to fit the wheels through the front door, and bump over the thing and get down the hall, and get through the door, and down the step into the kitchen. And we will have the cake on the table, and he'll read "welcome hom" and we'll say "Eeeee," and he'll know that means home. Welcome home.

RACHEL: How's he going to go upstairs?

MADISON: Don't know. He'll ride his crocodile.

RACHEL: Crocodiles are afraid of stairs.

MADISON: Crocodiles are afraid of rugs.

RACHEL: If you touch the rug, you die.

(Rachel jumps up on her chair.)

MADISON: If you touch the rug, your toes fall off.

(Madison climbs up on the table.)

RACHEL: Why do your toes fall off?

MADISON: If you touch the rug, the crocodiles eat your feet.

MADISON: How do we get to the fridge?

MADISON: You can touch the blue bits on the rug. The blue bits are the backs of the crocodiles, and you can touch them. The black bits are their icky teeth, and they eat your feet.

RACHEL: Eat your feet, eat your feet!

MADISON: Go get the cake.

RACHEL: You get the cake.

MADISON: There is no cake. The crocodiles ate it all up.

RACHEL: No, they didn't.

MADISON: Go take a look if you don't believe me.

(Rachel starts to get down.)

MADISON: Careful! Blue bits.

RACHEL: Okay.

(Rachel carefully picks her way across the rug on tiptoes.)

MADISON: Look out! He almost got you!

RACHEL: I saw! It moved — but I moved too.

MADISON: You're doing good.

RACHEL: Madison?

MADISON: Yeah?

RACHEL: Are there crocodiles in Iraq?

MADISON: Not in a helicopter.

RACHEL: Okay.

(A moment.)

MADISON: Come back.

RACHEL: I can reach the fridge.

MADISON: Come back to the table. Where it's safe.

RACHEL: I wanna see the cake.

MADISON: The cake's fine. Crocodiles never go inside fridges.

RACHEL: Or helicopters.

MADISON: Or helicopters. Come back.

RACHEL: I can reach the fridge.

MADISON: There's too many black bits. Sit on the table with me.

RACHEL: If I get to the cake, the crocodiles have to go away.

MADISON: They don't go away.

RACHEL: Yes, they do! They run away.

MADISON: When you get to the fridge, the crocodiles eat your feet. There's too many black bits.

RACHEL: Then I jump over them, and get back on the table.

MADISON: They climb up on the table. They climb out of the rug, and up on the chairs and up on the stairs and all over everywhere.

RACHEL: Stop it.

MADISON: They go inside helicopters.

RACHEL: You're scaring me.

MADISON: They've got teeth.

RACHEL: QUIT IT! Just stop!

> *(Beat. Madison jumps off the table, and holds Rachel in her arms.)*

MADISON: It's okay. It's okay. There's no crocodiles. It's a game. It's just a game.

RACHEL: I don't want to play anymore.

MADISON: When Daddy's here, we'll have cake.

RACHEL: He can't get in.

MADISON: Yes, he can. That's why there's a ramp. He can roll right up it.

RACHEL: He's not coming home.

MADISON: Yes he is. He'll pick you up, and put you on his lap, and spin around and around.

RACHEL: On his lap.

MADISON: Yeah. And we'll have cake. It will be a big party, and everyone on the whole world will come.

RACHEL: And the moon?

MADISON: Everyone on the moon will come too.

RACHEL: And no crocodiles?

MADISON: No. There's no crocodiles allowed.

RACHEL: They stay in Iraq.

MADISON: Okay.

RACHEL: It will be a big party.

MADISON: It will be a celebration.

RACHEL: When Daddy comes home.

MADISON: Any minute. Any minute now.

(They watch out of the window. Lights slowly fade. End of play.)

The Author Speaks

What inspired you to write this play?
Sacrifices made by soldiers are also made by their families. At the time the play was written, there was very little attention being paid to the soldiers returning from Iraq, there was a media blackout on the casualties of the war. I was a helicopter Instructor Pilot for the army when the invasion of Iraq occurred, and I was torn between wanting the public to be aware of the true cost of the war, and not wanting to see the death of young men used as a political tool. Of course, the decision to conceal their deaths was equally politically motivated. This play grew from that inner tension.

Was the structure of the play influenced by any other work?
No. Most of my plays follow a fairly formal structure—this one is much more freewheeling. It takes its structure from the ebb and flow of a children's game, just as the two young characters in it do.

Have you dealt with the same theme in other works that you have written?
I have—both in concrete form in a very personal piece, *Mopping the Stage*, which directly addressed my decision to work for the Army after the attacks of 9/11/2001 and my gradual change of heart when we engaged (to my mind) the wrong country entirely; but also in several other pieces (most notably *The Bricklayer*) which illustrate broader questions about guilt and responsibility.

What writers have had the most profound effect on your style?
I love the way Edward Albee and Tracy Letts handle dysfunctional family relationships, and David Mamet's musical rhythm to his dialogue...but I'm still affected by the lessons learned from my high school creative writing teacher.

You may have heard of him; he retired the year I graduated to write a book about his childhood in Ireland (*Angela's Ashes* by Frank McCourt).

What do you hope to achieve with this work?
This play is not a political diatribe, it doesn't advocate one position over another—it's not anti-war or jingoistic. It's a small play that highlights the wide nature of sacrifice, something I think gets overlooked sometimes. I want the audience to appreciate the unseen effects of war, and the men and women—and children—that bear some of those hidden costs.

What are the most common mistakes that occur in productions of your work?
I saw a rehearsal once where two actors had been struggling to find a moment. They knew it was there, but the scene wasn't working. After trying it a half dozen ways, the director suggested taking a long—and meaningful—pause before a key line. It worked. It was also in the script all along, described as "a deadly pause." Theatre is collaborative, you have to make it your own... but in a well written play, everything is there for a reason. An ellipsis or a dash makes all the difference to the delivery of a line. The days when elaborate, detailed stage directions ("she crosses S.L") were added by the stage manager are long gone. In a modern play the stage directions are used sparingly, and added by the playwright only when necessary. The director that crosses them out does so at their peril. Know the punctuation conventions in playwriting, and try the line as it actually is first...it's usually right.

What inspired you to become a playwright?
I've written my whole life, in numerous genres. I've had some success with fiction, magazine articles and screenplays, but my very first attempt at a play was produced at the Miami Summer Shorts Festival. Seeing several hundred people

reacting emotionally, alive and in the moment, to the words I had written fixed me on this career.

Do any films/videos exist of prior productions of this play?
There is a video on you-tube of the very first staged reading of the play by Theatre SouthWest in Houston. An animated screen version is currently in development by DVA Productions—and hopefully will be available by the time you read this.

Shakespeare gave advice to the players in *Hamlet*; if you could give advice to your cast what would it be?
If you talk to someone who's deeply worried about something, they'll often say they are fine, and nothing's wrong...while they drum their fingers on the table, or nervously fidget with their clothing or hair. That's what's going on here, the two young girls are playing games just like drumming their fingers. If you asked them what's wrong, they'd say "nothing" because they don't want to think about it. Use that physicality. Find the place where your fingers want to drum without you knowing why.

How was the first production different from the vision that you created in your mind?
The first production was performed by two sisters, a very talented actress Andrea Gauthier and her older sister the well known comedienne Renee Gauthier. Having two adults—and one of them a stand-up comic—playing at being little girls worked surprisingly well and brought the humor level way up, but I've always wanted to see it performed by a pair of age appropriate actors who happen to have the same level of talent. It might take a while!

About the Author

Arthur M. Jolly was recognized by the Academy of Motion Picture Arts and Sciences with a Nicholl Fellowship in Screenwriting, and is the playwright of more than sixty produced plays, including *A Gulag Mouse, Past Curfew, Trash, A Very Modern Marriage, The Ithaca Ladies Read Medea,* and *The Lady Demands Satisfaction.* He is a three-time Joining Sword and Pen winner, Todd McNerney National Playwriting Award winner, and a finalist for the Woodward/Newman Drama Award. His plays published by YouthPLAYS include *Rising, Long Joan Silver, What the Well Dressed Girl is Wearing, Snakes in a Lunchbox, Bully Issues, How Blue is My Crocodile, Moby (No Last Name Given), Bath Time is Fun Time* and *The Christmas Princess.* Jolly travels extensively, and is always happy to talk to classes and drama clubs about writing. He is repped by the Brant Rose Agency. Upcoming productions and contact info at www.arthurjolly.com.

MATH PROBLEMS
by Annie Harrison Elliott

CAST OF CHARACTERS

SARAH, female, math club whiz.

HENRY, male, best friends with Sarah, math club whiz.

MILES, male, self-proclaimed math genius.

MIA, female, secret math club whiz.

PAUL, male, leader of math club.

CHORUS OF 3+, any gender, math club students.

NOTE: Chorus lines should be variously assigned to meet the needs of each cast.

SETTING

An elementary school math club.

SPECIAL THANKS

Nicole B. Adkins & Laura King.

DEDICATION

For Morgan

(Lights up on an elementary school math club, including club leader PAUL and members SARAH, HENRY, MILES and MIA. A CHORUS of other math club students joins them.)

PAUL: Get your pencils ready. This is the most difficult question we've dared undertake here at Math Club —

CHORUS: *(Variously:)* Whoa./ Exciting./ Get ready.

HENRY & SARAH: *(Overenthusiastically:)* The special challenge question!

(Mia rolls her eyes.)

PAUL: Whoever solves this special problem first is the smartest of the smart. The best of the best. A math *genius.*

MILES: I'm totally a math genius —

HENRY & SARAH: It'll be epic!

(Henry creates a sound effect for the epic-ness.)

CHORUS: *(Variously:)* Ow./ That hurt./ My ears.

PAUL: For regional competition, I need the best of the best. There's one spot remaining on my Mathalon team. Whoever solves —

(Sarah creates a sound effect for the epic-ness.)

CHORUS: *(Variously:)* What?/ That's loud./ My ears.

MIA: I can't hear!

(The room gets quiet.)

PAUL: Whoever solves the special challenge question first will get the final spot on the competition team.

SARAH: I'm gonna win!

(Sarah starts singing her own victory theme song. She walks or dances around the room acting triumphant.)

Don't you love my victory song?

MILES: You got last week's WRONG!

SARAH: No. I won.

HENRY: She did.

PAUL: It's time to start—

HENRY: Hey, I *could* win—

(*He also sings his own kind of victory theme song and walks around the room triumphantly.*)

MIA: Can we please start now?

PAUL: Steve's father is 45—

(*No one responds. Henry continues his victory song. Sarah starts her victory song again in friendly competition with Henry.*)

(*Miles rolls his eyes.*)

MIA: I can't hear!

CHORUS: (*Variously:*) What?/ That's loud./ My ears.

(*The room gets quiet.*)

PAUL: Steve's father is 45. He is 15 years older than twice Steve's age—

MILES: Here it comes!

PAUL: How.old.is.Steve? On your mark.

HENRY: (*Bouncing up and down loudly:*) I can't wait!

PAUL: Get set.

SARAH: (*Bouncing up and down loudly:*) I can't wait!

MIA: I can't hear—

PAUL: GO!

(The students write furiously. Mia clearly finishes first. She looks around the room. She raises her hand, but Paul doesn't see it. Rather than yell out, she lowers her hand.)

SARAH & HENRY: DONE!

(Miles overdramatically acts like he's been wounded, falling to the floor in defeat.)

MILES: NOOOOOOOOOO!!!!!!!!!!!

SARAH & HENRY: *(Jumping up and down with joy:)* YAY! Yeah! Woo—

CHORUS: *(Variously:)* No./ Ah man./ So close.

MILES: We get it. You're happy.

SARAH & HENRY: *(Jumping up and down for joy:)* We did it! We did it—

MIA: We get it.

(Paul grabs their papers and studies them.)

PAUL: But are they correct?

(Paul squints at their work.)

SARAH: I assigned a variable to what we're supposed to find—

HENRY: Steve's age—

SARAH: Since X is Steve's age, and X equals 15—

HENRY: Steve is 15 years old.

PAUL: I declare…a tie!

(Sarah and Henry each do their victory songs, dances, or walks of triumph.)

MILES: *(Directed at Sarah, but not Henry:)* The rest of us are still smart! *(To Paul:)* Can we get back to math now?

CHORUS: *(Variously:)* Please./ Yes./ Hooray.

SARAH: I can't wait for Mathalon!

HENRY: It'll be epic!

MIA: Wait. If it's a tie, who gets the spot?

MILES: There's only one.

PAUL: I didn't think of that.

MILES: Rematch. Rematch. Rematch—

PAUL: Let's take a vote.

> *(Pause.)*

Voting is always fair. Right?

> *(They all shrug, including Chorus.)*

How many votes for Sarah?

> *(Possibly some Chorus members raise their hands.)*

Henry?

> *(Mia and Miles raise their hands, along with some Chorus.)*
>
> *(Whatever the Chorus breakdown is, make sure Henry is clearly the winner.)*
>
> *(Sarah looks crushed. This bothers Henry.)*

HENRY: Guys. I don't know. Are we sure this is fair?

SARAH: I win the special challenge questions a lot. More than Henry. Why didn't you vote for me?

MIA: You're loud.

> *(Chorus looks at each other.)*

SARAH: *(Re: Henry:)* So is he.

> *(Chorus reacts.)*

MIA: Not as loud as you.

SARAH: That's not true! And you still voted for him!

MIA: He always wins the special challenge questions.

SARAH: But I win more.

HENRY: *(A realization:)* Actually…she *does.*

(Chorus reacts.)

MIA: You gloat more.

(Chorus reacts.)

MILES: I agree!

SARAH: No. I don't.

MIA: You do.

SARAH: Not more than Henry!

MIA: It's more annoying when you do it.

SARAH: Seriously?!

PAUL: Henry's a leader.

SARAH: But why am I not—

MILES: *(Trying to be helpful…not realizing he's hurtful:)* You don't act right.

(Chorus reacts.)

(Pause.)

SARAH: What do you mean?

MIA: You're too silly.

SARAH: I act the *same* way as Henry. I'm excited about math. That's all!

MIA: It seems fake.

PAUL: No one can hear me when you're singing. It's annoying.

SARAH: I'm not trying to be…annoying.

HENRY: I'm really loud, guys.

(Chorus considers this.)

SARAH: What did I do?

HENRY: Sarah always knows the answer. You'll need her on the team to win—

MILES: You only think that cuz you LOOVE her—

CHORUS: *(Variously:)* Whoa./ Really?/ Called it!

HENRY: Eww. *No.* We're best friends.

SARAH: We both sang victory songs.

PAUL: He's just excited about math!

SARAH: Were you listening to me at all?

(Chorus considers.)

MILES: Maybe you should change how you act.

(Chorus takes a unison inhale.)

(Pause.)

SARAH: Okay.

(Pause.)

Am I really that loud?

MILES: People might vote for you…if you act…differently.

SARAH: Okay.

(Pause.)

I'll sit down. And be quiet. Just like Mia.

(She sits for a moment, in silence. This really bothers Mia.)

But don't you think I act the exact *same* as Henry?

PAUL: This isn't a word problem.

SARAH: If this *were* a special challenge question…I'd be asking myself what the variable is—

MIA: There's a difference between competitive and *gloating*.

(Sarah gives Mia a look.)

Your voice is louder!

SARAH: Ugh. It's not!

HENRY: Seriously. She can't be louder than me. I'm really loud, guys.

PAUL: Actually, that could be true. Look at his big mouth.

(Henry nods enthusiastically and makes an "aaahhh" sound while opening his mouth.)

(Chorus reacts.)

MILES: What if you both screamed at the same time?

(Chorus considers.)

SARAH: What?

MILES: See who's louder. Paul can judge.

MIA: That's dumb.

SARAH: No. Let's do it!

MIA: Why?

SARAH: Because I'm tired of *you* telling me how loud I am!

MIA: Someone could hear. We'll all get in trouble.

SARAH: Are you scared to be wrong?

MIA: *No.*

SARAH: Okay, then.

PAUL: On my mark.

(Pause.)

GO!

(Henry and Sarah scream together at the same decibel, or they could create a harmonized note or sound.)

CHORUS: *(Variously:)* Woah./ My ears./ Impressive./ Not bad.

HENRY: See? No one's louder than me, guys.

PAUL: They sound the same. Right?

(Mia nods. Chorus nods.)

SARAH: See?

MILES: This doesn't make sense.

MIA: Yeah.

(Pause.)

HENRY: Sarah should be on the team. She wins more. I'll resign. She can have my spot—

SARAH: No.

HENRY: Why?

SARAH: No one will believe I deserve it. Miles was right—

MILES: I'm right!

SARAH: About a *rematch*. Paul. Ask us an even harder question.

PAUL: *(Nervous:)* What's harder than the special challenge question I already asked?

SARAH: If I beat everyone in this room, it'll prove I'm the best of the best. That I deserve the spot. *Miles?*

MILES: Game. ON.

PAUL: *(Consulting a Mathalon book:)* Okay…there's a super hard problem in the Mathalon practice manual.

(Pause.)

We'll solve a one-step variable *inequality.*

(Everyone including Chorus nods.)

MILES: *(Bragging:)* Everyone might not understand the definition. An inequality is a relation that holds between two values when they are different—

SARAH: We all get it!

PAUL: Step one is to identify the variable. Ready?

(Everyone including Chorus nods.)

On your mark—

SARAH: *(Lightbulb moment:)* I know the answer!

MILES: We haven't even heard the question—

SARAH: I've been trying to prove Henry and I are the same. I've been asking the wrong thing.

MILES: Huh?

SARAH: This isn't just about finding a variable. This is a variable *inequality.* And an inequality is a relation that holds between two values when they are *different.*

HENRY: They think you're loud, but I'm just excited. They think you're gloating, but I'm a leader. They think I'm better at math because— *(A realization:)* they treat me differently.

SARAH: I've identified the variable—

MIA: *(A realization:)* You're a girl.

(A moment between them.)

SARAH: Congratulations. You've solved for X.

MIA: I knew the answer to the special challenge question too.

SARAH: What?

MIA: But I didn't want to yell out—

HENRY: You finished before we did?

SARAH: You should have said something!

MIA: I know.

SARAH: It seems like you know the answers a lot, but then you never say anything—

MIA: People might think I'm gloating!

SARAH: But you're the one who says *I'm* gloating!

MIA: I didn't realize what I was doing.

> *(Pause:)*

Truthfully, I'm tired of sitting still and being quiet when I don't want to be.

MILES: Ugh. Are you going to start acting all differently now?

> *(Pause.)*

MIA: Yes.

> *(Pause.)*

I'm sorry, Sarah.

SARAH: Thank you.

> *(Pause.)*

To be fair…I guess the spot is yours.

PAUL: What if there's another solution—

CHORUS: *(Variously:)* What?/ Tell us./ Please.

PAUL: *(Looking at the Mathalon book:)* It states here we can send more than one team.

> *(Pause.)*

We could send my team and…Sarah's team?

SARAH: My team?

PAUL: You win the most special challenge questions. It seems fair.

MILES: What are you talking about? Voting is always fair!

SARAH: Mia and Henry can join?

PAUL: You're the leader.

SARAH: *(Jumping up and down:)* I can't wait for Mathalon!

CHORUS: *(Variously:)* Yes!/ Hooray!/ Let's start.

MIA: *(Yelling loudly:)* IT'LL BE EPIC!

(Everyone pauses, startled by Mia's new voice. Everyone but Miles breaks into smiles and laughter.)

(End of play.)

The Author Speaks

What inspired you to write this play?

Starting in middle school, I began to feel like math was a subject that was closed to me. No one ever explicitly said that, "girls aren't good at math," but it was nevertheless the message I received subliminally through media, my peers, and even teachers. This false belief I inherited impacted me greatly. And I missed out on what I now understand is a really cool subject! I wanted to write a play that would allow students to think critically about the issue of gender and math.

Was the structure or other elements of the play influenced by any other work?

I was inspired by a lot of the research I did on girls and math. The reading I did illuminated something I already knew from my own experience—that the achievement gap between girls and boys in the subject of math is due to socialization, not ability. I wanted to represent this idea dramatically, which is how I developed the character of Mia. Following my research process, I found the structure of the play as I wrote. The notes I received from YouthPLAYS and other writers really helped me shape the play's trajectory and commit to a consistent style. I also decided I wanted it to be a little bit funny, even though the subject matter is "serious." When I see a play, I always want to laugh, at least a little bit. I aimed for the style of this piece to allow for both comedy and deep thought.

Have you dealt with the same theme in other works that you have written?

Yes. Many of my plays deal with the issue of gender parity, or women working in science or technology fields. My play *Empty Rooms* is about a female computer programmer and the problems she faces being the only woman in the room. *General Gabler's Daughter* is an adaptation of the play *Hedda*

Gabler, in which the protagonist is a former astro-biologist who feels forced out of the workplace. ***Beauty & The Boss*** grapples with the gender parity problem implicit in the telling of many children's stories. My plays generally grapple with these themes by examining and unpacking the idea of unconscious bias. I am interested in the insidious nature of our conditioning when it comes to gender parity. The complexity of the issue interests me greatly, which allows me to return to the subject again and again.

What writers have had the most profound effect on your style?
I've been influenced by the writing of Lynn Nottage, Margaret Edson, Suzan Lori-Parks, Caridad Svich, Henrik Ibsen, Kristoffer Diaz, Lauren Gunderson, Christopher Durang, and others. I am also consistently influenced by my playwright friends and colleagues whom I collaborate with on a regular basis.

What do you hope to achieve with this work?
I would like to raise awareness about gender parity and math. If girls (or boys) have internalized this double standard without knowing it, I hope this play gets them asking questions and interrogating their own belief systems. I also hope they have fun performing it! I am very excited to see how each student choreographs their very own victory dance!

What were the biggest challenges involved in the writing of this play?
This was the first play I wrote for elementary school-age children, and it was challenging! It took a lot of rewriting to get the right balance of delivering the message without being too "preachy." That said, I think I learned more writing this play than I often do while writing for adults. I also needed to relearn some algebra, and that was daunting at first. As I read through each word problem, I realized I'm clearly still

working through my own false beliefs about my math abilities. Gah! I'm 35. I thought my math fear was over. In the end, I'm glad I dived back into algebra, and I have resolved to revisit the subject more often.

What are the most common mistakes that occur in productions of your work?

Even though the play is "about" gender parity, it's still just like any other play that doesn't center around an "issue." The story matters. When the "issue" starts to take over the work, that can be a problem. Also, just because the topic is serious, that doesn't mean the play can't be funny, or even have hilarious moments.

What inspired you to become a playwright?

I've been writing stories since I was a kid. I started out as an actor, but quickly became disillusioned with the profession. I majored in Creative Writing, and I realized that playwriting was a way I could combine my love of acting and writing without actually having to be an actor. I love the creative control I get as a writer. I also love being able to create entire worlds by using my imagination. In addition, I like the idea of hopefully creating nuanced female roles for actors.

How did you research the subject?

I researched articles and statistics on girls and math. Then, I researched the math problems themselves, as well as elementary school math clubs and mathalons.

Are any characters modeled after real life or historical figures?

No. But a lot of the characters are named after my son's friends.

What is your writing process?

I honestly have no idea. Haha! It changes from project to project. I do usually start working on an idea from a personal place, and then I grow it through research. My first drafts are usually terrible. I rewrite a lot, but luckily I like rewriting. I used to hate outlining, but lately I'm really into it. And color coding. And index cards. I am often inspired to create interesting female protagonists by watching the women I see in my daily life, or from reading about women from history.

Shakespeare gave advice to the players in *Hamlet*; if you could give advice to your cast what would it be?
Have fun! Enjoy these characters. Support each other, both onstage and off. Believe in yourselves. Trust your instincts.

About the Author

Annie Harrison Elliott has taught theatre to children of all ages as a teaching artist in New York City, Pennsylvania, and Atlanta. As a playwright, her work has been developed, commissioned, or produced by: Alliance Theatre, Actor's Express, Atlanta History Center, Found Stages, Wide Eyed Productions NYC, Weird Sister's Theatre Project, Working Title Playwrights, and others. She is the recipient of the Reiser Artist Lab Award from Alliance Theatre, and her play **Empty Rooms** was a Eugene O'Neill Semi-Finalist. She holds a BA in Creative Writing from Franklin & Marshall College, and a Master's from New York University. Her essays, Op-Eds, and poems have been published by *The Teaching Artist Journal*, *Huffington Post*, and *N/A Literary Journal*. She is currently developing a comedy TV series with Picture It Productions. Annie is a member of the Dramatists Guild and Writers Guild of America East.

MESSAGE TO GRANDMA
by Claudia Haas

CAST OF CHARACTERS

LUKE, male, 9-10, introspective determined young man on a mission.

MEGAN, female, 11, Luke's sister; "old" for her age.

SAM, any gender, 11, fun-loving neighbor.

JAMIE, any gender, 10, Sam's younger sibling; the world is magical.

SETTING

A garden.

TIME

Summer, today. Dusk.

(We are in a huge backyard garden. We spy LUKE there. He is very busy. He has a glass jar containing a dragonfly. He also has a flashlight and a balloon. Luke speaks to the dragonfly in the jar.)

LUKE: Not to worry, Lancelot. I'll have you out very soon. You are about to go on a very important mission. Don't bat those beautiful, dragonfly wings at me! I promise I'll let you go. I'd do a pinky swear with you if you had—you know—a pinky. I need to prepare everything first. Don't do that! If you bang your head against the glass you could cause brain damage. I mean—you must have a little brain to fit inside that tiny head. Just rest. Yes, rest.

(MEGAN enters from her home.)

MEGAN: Luke? Luke! What are you doing out here? The mosquitoes are biting. Come inside.

LUKE: Not so loud. You'll scare Lancelot.

MEGAN: Oh, no! I turn my back for one minute and you find a new imaginary friend! Mom will never let me babysit you again!

LUKE: Lancelot's real, Megan. See for yourself.

MEGAN: Ohhh! Poor little dragonfly. Let him go!

LUKE: I will. In a minute. He's going on a top-secret mission.

(Some rustling is heard.)

MEGAN: What's that?

LUKE: What?

(Rustling is heard again.)

MEGAN: That! Come on, Luke. It's weird out here when Mom and Dad aren't home.

(SAM enters.)

SAM: Spooked you, didn't I?

MEGAN: Sam! What're you doing here?

SAM: Spooking you!

MEGAN: I wasn't spooked a bit.

SAM: Yeah, you were. Totally.

MEGAN: Just the tiniest bit—agitated. That's all. Now—leave!

SAM: Way to welcome a neighbor!

MEGAN: I'm in charge and my mom and dad said no visitors.

SAM: I'm not a visitor—I'm an intruder.

MEGAN: Go!

(Meanwhile, Luke is busy putting a note inside a balloon and then trying to blow up the balloon.)

JAMIE: Sam! Ohhh, Sammy!

SAM: Hide me!

MEGAN: Over here, Jamie!

SAM: You're just out to get me, aren't you? Now I'll have to deal with Jamie.

MEGAN: She's [He's] your sister [brother].

SAM: Don't remind me!

JAMIE: Why'd you leave me?

SAM: I didn't leave you. I took a stroll. Over the fence.

JAMIE: The leaves were whispering to me. I wanted you to hear them.

SAM: I'm telling you—it's like living in a fairy tale with that one!

JAMIE: And then there was this shadow that looked like a giant dragon and it was right on top of me!

SAM: Why didn't you go to Mom?

JAMIE: She'd tell me I was being silly.

SAM: And so you are. I am never, ever camping in the yard with you again!

LUKE: *Would you all go somewhere else and argue? You're ruining my concentration.*

MEGAN: Luke! Just come inside now! *And you – go home!*

LUKE: I can't come in yet. No use asking me. I have to finish this.

MEGAN: Finish it inside!

LUKE: Can't!

MEGAN: *Won't!*

SAM: Don't fight, children.

JAMIE: What are you doing to that poor dragonfly?

LUKE: Nothing.

JAMIE: Something!

LUKE: *Would you all please go away?*

MEGAN: Luke...you can tell me...

SAM: Yes, Luke. You can tell *us* anything.

LUKE: Well, if you must know, I'm sending a message to Grandma.

(*Silence as the other three look at each other.*)

MEGAN: Luke...you do understand Grandma's gone, don't you? And she's not coming back.

LUKE: Megan! I'm not a baby! I know she's...passed on.

SAM: Are...you planning a séance or something?

LUKE: It's more scientific than that.

(Megan emits a small scream.)

Don't do that—you'll scare Lancelot.

MEGAN: There was a creepy-crawly thing on me. Come on, Luke, please go inside!

SAM: There's a creepy-crawling thing over there.

MEGAN: Where?

SAM: There!

(Megan squeals again.)

LUKE: Stop doing that! *(Looks at Lancelot:)* It's okay, Lancelot. I'm going to let you go in a sec.

SAM: You named the dragonfly?

LUKE: He's my messenger. You know—to talk to Grandma.

JAMIE: He's a talking dragonfly?

MEGAN: Whoa! You are in serious need of some head-checking. There is no evidence that insects can talk to the dead.

LUKE: I'm just letting him fly up to the heavens tonight and find Grandma. I showed him pictures and he knows what to do. I want him to help Grandma remember me. She knows I love dragonflies.

JAMIE: People don't have bodies in heaven. How would he know which floating soul is your Grandma?

LUKE: I sang Grandma's favorite hymn to him. You know that Grandma will be singing in Heaven.

MEGAN: Yeah, she would.

SAM: How can you sing without a body? That doesn't make sense.

LUKE: You're in Heaven! You don't have to make sense! Now, everyone leave me alone and let me finish.

SAM: So, what's all the other stuff for? The balloon and the flashlight?

LUKE: Well, I have this message—see? *(Pulling out a tiny crumpled piece of paper:)* And I'm going to stick it in this balloon and let it float to Heaven.

MEGAN: You can't do that. 'Cause of the birds. The balloon could get caught on power lines and in trees and strangle the birds.

LUKE: Are you sure?

SAM: Besides, only helium balloons go to Heaven. It's a well-known fact.

LUKE: Well, then I have other stuff. Like the flashlight!

MEGAN: Luke—how is the flashlight going to send a message to Grandma?

LUKE: Well, you turn it on and it sends a beam of light through the sky. Maybe Grandma will see it. And she'll think, "Oh, that's Luke down there." And she'll remember what she promised.

MEGAN: Promised?

LUKE: Yeah. She promised that after she died—she would come back and tell us how it was—you know—up there.

SAM: So why don't you just talk to her?

LUKE: I tried that. But she never answered.

SAM: You know—maybe she didn't hear you. Maybe another grandma heard you and was confused. My grandma gets confused sometimes.

JAMIE: I don't think there's anyone in charge of messages up there. I think they just play harps and sing all day.

LUKE: I have to try, okay? Could you blow up the balloon for me and we'll attach this message to it—and Sam can turn the flashlight on and I'll let Lancelot out of his jar and we'll see what happens. Come on—what are we waiting for?

(The kids do so.)

MEGAN: What's the message say?

LUKE: It's just—well, I told her it was okay if she forgot to come back and talk to me. But I wanted her to know that I didn't forget her. I'll never forget her.

(Megan has the balloon, Sam has the flashlight. Luke opens the jar and the dragonfly "flies away" during this. You do not need a real dragonfly. The actors can make this happen.)

Okay. On my count. Grandma! We're sending a message. Grandma! Are you listening? Okay. One...two...three...GO!

(The balloon flies away, Lancelot is let out of the jar [you may imagine] and the flashlight is turned on to the sky. They quietly watch each action.)

MEGAN: The dragonfly went to a plant, Luke.

SAM: The balloon's never going to make it.

LUKE: I had everything planned. The light...the dragonfly...the balloon...the message...Well, I guess that's that. Grandma's never going to get the message.

MEGAN: I don't know, Luke. Maybe you're just not hearing her.

JAMIE: My grandma says that sometimes when the wind blows, she hears her mom calling—like when she was a little kid.

MEGAN: Grandma loved this garden. She planted those daisies for me...And those over there are for you.

LUKE: I know. That's why I thought if I did all this in the garden—she'd notice.

MEGAN: *(Looking at the sky:)* Wow! Did you see that?

LUKE: That cloud is moving real fast.

SAM: No. It's growing. The cloud is actually growing! Weird. We'd better go in. Something's happening up there.

JAMIE: It is amazing—how the cloud keeps changing its shape. It looks like a harp—

LUKE: No—it's a face! See the nose?

MEGAN: Wow! It's smiling! The cloud is smiling! Look, Luke!

LUKE: Can she see us? We're in the garden, Grandma! Can you see? We're in the garden.

> *(Megan and Luke may give each other an awkward hug and wave at the sky as the lights dim.)*

> *(Blackout. End of play.)*

The Author Speaks

What inspired you to write this play?
I had two losses fairly close together. One was "expected," even though not welcomed. The other was a shock. As family and friends come together for comfort, many things are said and done to help each other. Although nobody tried what Luke tried to do, there were some inspiring ways found to keep those who passed—still close.

Was the structure or other elements of the play influenced by any other work?
Luke's way of trying to reach his grandma in heaven has a bit of magical realism in it. This is an approach that I have used a lot in the past few years. I like it because it is theatrical. I love it because there's a wide-open universe out there. We have some answers but not all, and you never know when the fancy turns into reality.

Have you dealt with the same theme in other works that you have written?
I certainly have dealt with grief a number of times and with the healing process. Luke's character is the youngest character I have written on this theme. Nobody escapes grief and all of us search for ways to keep loved ones forever in our hearts. Most of my plays come from a touched nerve and a question. Writing about loss and healing helps me answer my own questions to myself. But of course the question will never be one hundred percent answered because there is the unknown and so I ask it again and again from different perspectives.

What writers have had the most profound effect on your style?
I don't know that I was consciously affected by another playwright's style. I do love and do write episodic plays and I can thank the wonderful Wendy Wasserstein for that. My

writing has evolved. My early commissions were all for young performers who wanted summer fun and there were a lot of comedic one-liners à la Neil Simon to fulfill that want. These days, I work with smaller casts, with characters that have bigger challenges and I search for more creative ways to build a character arc.

What do you hope to achieve with this work?

I would love the audiences to "nod their head" and understand Luke's need. I want them able to put themselves into Luke's place and feel gladness at the end of the play. I hope the young actors who portray the characters can discuss the impact of loss. And I hope that both the audience and the actors can appreciate the coming together of all the characters at the end of the play.

What were the biggest challenges involved in the writing of this play?

I write predominantly for older teens. There is a need for work for elementary school ages and I wanted to write something for the youngest of actors. I have done a lot of folk tales and fairy tales for young actors and young audiences. I wanted to address other subjects and write something for them that was not a "ha-ha" comedy. I worked on what would be in the realm of the character's experience. It's a different world than that of the sixteen-year-old. The sixteen-year-old characters and dialogue come a lot easier to me.

What are the most common mistakes that occur in productions of your work?

I don't see enough of my productions to accurately answer this. The ones that I have seen were pretty spot-on. I did miss one local production where the producing theatre thought I would be excited to see "the chase scene with 45 characters." The play did not have a chase scene and had 28 characters. I was sick and couldn't go, but I remain curious.

What inspired you to become a playwright?
I was born with the theatre gene. I went into acting and segued into teaching and directing. It took me awhile to learn that I wanted to write the words—not "say" them. I started writing to address the needs of my teens in my acting classes. Most plays that were royalty-free (I had no budget) did not address the reality of the teen classes and teen acting programs—which is 75-80% female and 20-25% male (if you're lucky). I started writing plays for my classes and could also write plays for specific actors and actresses in mind. The plays took on a life of their own, and through this happenstance, I became a playwright.

How did you research the subject?
The play required no research. It required me going into the minds of children as they seek to connect to heaven and in doing so—connect to each other. The play was a brainstorm I had sitting in my yard watching the night sky. I wrote it in my head sitting outside and rushed inside to get it on paper.

Are any characters modeled after real life or historical figures?
The characters are all fictional. They are inspired by the many children in my personal and work life. Over the years, I have seen children deal with loss in creative and poignant ways. I wrote this after some losses in my life, noting how younger people were handling the same loss. We all find comfort in different ways.

Shakespeare gave advice to the players in Hamlet; if you could give advice to your cast what would it be?
The characters truly like each other. The task at hand is very important to Luke. Nothing will dissuade him.

About the Author

Claudia Haas has over fifty published plays with over 1100 productions in every state in the US as well as on five continents. Awards include: Old Miner's Children's Playwriting Contest (***Almost Mary***), Unpublished Play Reading Project (***La Bella Cinderella***), Prince George's Children's Theatre Play Writing Contest (***La Bella Cinderella*** and ***The Fisherman and His Wife***), East Valley Children's Theatre Play Writing Contest (*Cap o' Rushes*), Playwrights in our Schools Grant (***Antigone in Munich*** and ***Under a Midsummer Moon***), Anna Zornio Memorial Playwrighting Competition (***The Fisherman and His Wife***), Purple Crayon Players Development Playground (***Bound by Stardust***), Aurand Harris Children's Playwrighting Competition (***By Candlelight***), Bonderman Symposium (now called "Write Now") (***By Candlelight***), The Jackie White Memorial Children's Play Writing Contest (twice: ***The Haunting of Will Shakespeare*** and ***Commedia Delight***). She is a member of the Dramatists Guild, Playwrights Center of Minneapolis and the American Alliance for Theatre Education. Website: www.claudiahaas.com.

THE CASE OF THE MISSING ROOSTER
by Anne Negri

CAST OF CHARACTERS

LEAD DETECTIVE

DETECTIVE'S ASSISTANT

RUSTY THE ROOSTER

HATTIE THE HEN

MR. BROWN

MRS. BROWN

SALLY BROWN

DANNY BROWN

MRS. EVICTION

JENNY EVICTION

JASPER EVICTION

RON THE ROOSTER TRAINER

COOK

COUNTY FAIR JUDGE

LIBRARIAN

FARM WORKER

THE ROOSTER ROOTERS

PERCY (or PENNY) JONES

LUCY (or LOUIS) PARTRIDGE

BETSY (or BENNY) CLARK

All of the characters are gender flexible. For a larger cast, additional performers may play The Rooster Rooters.

(A rooster crows loudly. The LEAD DETECTIVE and DETECTIVE'S ASSISTANT enter sneaking around as if they are looking for clues. The Detective notices the audience and stops suddenly. The Assistant, who was following close behind bumps into the Detective.)

DETECTIVE: Watch where you're going!

ASSISTANT: Sorry.

(Assistant takes out a notebook and takes notes on what the Detective is saying.)

DETECTIVE: *(To the audience:)* Ahem! I am the Town Detective and this is my Assistant. We do all of our detective work in Tinytown USA, population 333. Many people assume that I don't do a lot of detective work in such a small town, but you would be very surprised. *(To Assistant:)* Right?

ASSISTANT: Very surprised.

DETECTIVE: In fact, Tinytown is a very busy place for detectives. *(To Assistant:)* Right?

ASSISTANT: Very busy.

DETECTIVE: Once in a while, we get a really hard case…one with dark deeds and sinister suspects. I'll tell you the story of Tinytown's toughest case to crack. *(Look to Assistant.)*

ASSISTANT: Very tough.

DETECTIVE: A case that will go down as one of the most fowl cases in the history of detecting!

DETECTIVE & ASSISTANT: The Case of the Missing Rooster!

(At the Brown family farm. It is the day before the County Fair and everyone is excitedly preparing Rusty the Rooster for the competition that he has won 1st place in ten years in a row.)

(MR. and MRS. BROWN enter.)

MRS. BROWN: Did you get Rusty's cage clean?

MR. BROWN: Sure did. Did you pack the bird feed?

MRS. BROWN: All set.

MR. BROWN: Shall we go check on Rusty?

MRS. BROWN: I'll call the kids. *(Yells:)* Sally! Danny!

(SALLY enters very excited. DANNY enters, not very excited.)

Shall we do our final check on Rusty before we leave for the fair tomorrow?

SALLY: Yes! I can't wait to go. I just know Rusty is going to win the blue ribbon again!

DANNY: Do I have to go?

MR. BROWN: Of course, Danny! This is a family tradition.

DANNY: I know…but I don't really feel like going this year.

MRS. BROWN: Why not?

DANNY: Well, first we have to go there in that gas-guzzling truck!

SALLY: You can ride your bike.

DANNY: But once I get to the fair, I won't be able to find anything to eat!

MRS. BROWN: When you decided to become a vegetarian, you knew it was going to be tough to do in Tinytown.

DANNY: I know! Every single salad at the restaurant has meat on it.

SALLY: You could pack a lunch before you leave.

DANNY: I guess I could do that.

(Knock on the door.)

SALLY: I'll get it! Maybe it's Rusty's Rooster Rooters!

(The ROOSTER ROOTERS enter cheering with signs. Sally joins in with them.)

ROOSTER ROOTERS: *(Chanting:)* Rusty, Rusty he's our bird! He would never come in third! Rusty, Rusty he can crow! He'll win first at the big show!

MR. BROWN: All right! Brown Family and Rusty Rooters, out to the barn!

(All exit. In the barn are RON THE ROOSTER TRAINER, FARM WORKER and RUSTY THE ROOSTER.)

RON THE ROOSTER TRAINER: Alright, Rusty…do you think you can jump up, spin around and crow as loud as you can?

RUSTY: Of course I can. Don't forget, I am a ten-time blue ribbon winner!

RON THE ROOSTER TRAINER: I didn't forget. I just want to make sure you are ready for your competition tomorrow.

RUSTY: I was born ready!

(Rusty performs the trick.)

RON THE ROOSTER TRAINER: Excellent, here's a treat!

RUSTY: *(Gobbles the treat.)* Dee-licious!

FARM WORKER: *(To Rusty:)* Should I prepare your roost for the evening?

RUSTY: *(Yawns.)* I am getting tired.

FARM WORKER: Big day tomorrow! Better get your beauty sleep.

(Farm Worker exits to make up Rusty's roost. The Brown Family and Rooster Rooters enter.)

ROOSTER ROOTERS: Look! It's Rusty! *(Chant:)* Rusty, Rusty he's the best! He is better than the rest!

(The Rooster Rooters run to Rusty and pet him.)

SALLY: *(To Ron:)* How is the training going?

RON THE ROOSTER TRAINER: He's great! *(Whispers to the family so Rusty can't hear:)* Maybe not as great as in past years, but I think he's got one more win in him.

SALLY: Only one more?

RON THE ROOSTER TRAINER: He is ten years old. That's pretty old for a rooster.

DANNY: What's going to happen to Rusty after that?

MRS. BROWN: Don't worry about that.

FARM WORKER: Everything is ready for you. Everyone needs to leave so Rusty can sleep.

MR. BROWN: Say goodnight, we have an early morning tomorrow!

EVERYONE: Goodnight, Rusty! Good luck tomorrow!

(All exit. Rusty yawns again and exits to sleep. Detective and Assistant enter and sit in two chairs that serve as their office.)

DETECTIVE: That's when we come in!

(The office phone rings.)

ASSISTANT: Detective's office? Hello Mr. Brown—how can we help you? Oh no!

DETECTIVE: What is it?

ASSISTANT: *(Into the phone:)* Right…right… OK.

DETECTIVE: What? What?

ASSISTANT: We'll be right over! *(Hangs up the phone.)* It's Rusty! He's...he's missing!

DETECTIVE: Oh no!

(The Detective and Assistant exit. At the Brown home, Mr. and Mrs. Brown, Sally, Danny and The Rooster Rooters are in the barn. The Rooster Rooters are crying.)

BETSY: How could this happen?

LUCY: Where could he be?

SALLY: Maybe he escaped?

PERCY: No, I think somebody took him!

(Knock at the door. Mrs. Brown answers the door, and the Detective and Assistant enter.)

DETECTIVE: We are so sorry to hear that Rusty has gone missing.

ASSISTANT: Very sorry.

DETECTIVE: Did you find any clues at the scene of the incident?

MRS. BROWN: The first clue was feathers. *(She holds up some loose feathers.)*

LUCY: *(Crying:)* We...we...we...also...found... *(Break down into sobs.)*

BETSY: A carrot.

DETECTIVE: A carrot! Possibly used to lure Rusty away.

ASSISTANT: What else did you find?

MR. BROWN: We found this page torn from a book.

(Mr. Brown hands the page to the Detective.)

DETECTIVE: Hmmm…looks like a page from an encyclopedia…about roosters. Interesting, right?

ASSISTANT: Very interesting.

DETECTIVE: *(To everyone:)* I have some ideas about who might have taken Rusty.

SALLY: Who?

DANNY: Yeah, who?

DETECTIVE: I would like to interview some people from Tinytown. Some are suspects and some possible witnesses.

(All exit except for the Detective and Assistant.)

First, the County Fair Judge: Character Witness.

(The COUNTY FAIR JUDGE enters.)

COUNTY FAIR JUDGE: I hope you two are going to find Rusty!

DETECTIVE: We're trying.

ASSISTANT: How do you know Rusty?

COUNTY FAIR JUDGE: Well, I'm the one who has given him every single one of his ten blue ribbons! He's the greatest bird I have ever judged.

DETECTIVE: Do you know anyone who would want to take Rusty?

COUNTY FAIR JUDGE: I really don't. Rusty has been an inspirational mascot for Tinytown for the last ten years. However, there is one family that might want to see him gone.

ASSISTANT: Who?

COUNTY FAIR JUDGE: The Evictions and their second place prize-winning hen, Hattie. They've been jealous of Rusty for years. They've written me several mean letters.

DETECTIVE: Thank you, Judge.

(The County Fair Judge exits. MRS. EVICTION, HATTIE, JENNY and JASPER enter.)

Mrs. Eviction, Jenny, and Jasper.

MRS. EVICTION: Yes?

ASSISTANT: And who's that? *(Points to Hattie.)*

HATTIE: I'm Hattie the Hen!

JASPER: Our prize-winning hen.

DETECTIVE: Oh really? So you must know Rusty the Rooster.

MRS. EVICTION: Rusty wins first place at the fair every year.

JENNY: Hattie always gets second place.

JASPER: It's not fair.

HATTIE: I'm just as good as him!

DETECTIVE: Did you know that Rusty has gone missing?

MRS. EVICTION: No, we didn't know!

JENNY: No, it wasn't me!

JASPER: Me neither.

HATTIE: I certainly didn't take him.

DETECTIVE: There were feathers at the scene of the crime.

MRS. EVICTION: They were probably Rusty's feathers. He is a bird, you know!

ASSISTANT: Very true.

DETECTIVE: When was the last time any of you saw Rusty?

MRS. EVICTION: I can tell you exactly the last time we saw him. *(The Evictions act this out as she tells the story.)* Two days ago, I sent Jenny and Jasper into the bird feed store with Hattie. When they got inside, they ran into Sally, Danny, and Rusty.

(Sally, Danny and Rusty enter the flashback.)

RUSTY: Hey Hattie! You ready to get your second-place ribbon again this year?

DANNY: Rusty, don't be rude.

HATTIE: We'll see. I might surprise you this year!

RUSTY: You got some new tricks?

JASPER: She sure does. I've been training her. Watch this!

(Hattie performs a cool trick.)

JENNY: Beat that, Rusty!

DANNY: Pretty good, but watch this!

(Rusty performs a trick.)

SALLY: Rusty rocks!

(Hattie and Rusty start to fight, but the children pull them apart.)

MRS. EVICTION: Then I went into the store. *(Mrs. Eviction enters the flashback:)* What's going on in here?

JENNY: They started it!

JASPER: Rusty was bragging, and then Hattie and Rusty got into a fight!

MRS. EVICTION: *(To Hattie:)* Are you alright my dear, sweet hen?

HATTIE: I'm guess I'm OK. That rude rooster tried to hurt me so that I would get disqualified!

MRS. EVICTION: *(To Danny and Sally:)* You keep that rooster away from Hattie…or else!

RUSTY: Or else what?!

SALLY & DANNY: Rusty!

MRS. EVICTION: *(To the Detectives:)* And that was the last time anyone from my family saw Rusty.

DETECTIVE: Thank you for your story.

ASSISTANT: We may be contacting you again.

(The Evictions exit.)

DETECTIVE: Who's next?

ASSISTANT: The Cook: Suspect!

(The COOK enters and approaches the detectives as if they are eating at his restaurant.)

COOK: Good afternoon, Detectives! Welcome to my restaurant. Our special today is roasted chicken with a side of red potatoes and cooked carrots.

DETECTIVE: A chicken special! With cooked carrots!

(The Detective holds up the baggie with the carrot evidence.)

COOK: Yes, it's a perfect dish. You two should try it.

ASSISTANT: Did you know that the Brown Family rooster, Rusty, has gone missing?

COOK: Oh no! That's too bad. I was hoping to watch Rusty win a blue ribbon today.

DETECTIVE: Are you sure you weren't hoping to put Rusty into your chicken special?!

COOK: Ha ha ha ha ha!

DETECTIVE: Why's he laughing? He must think we're joking, but we're not—we're serious. Right?

ASSISTANT: Very serious!

COOK: I'm sorry, but it's so funny! Why would I want a ten-year-old rooster for my chicken special? Rusty would be one tough chicken to eat!

(The Cook exits, laughing.)

ASSISTANT: The Librarian: Suspect!

(The LIBRARIAN enters.)

DETECTIVE: How do you feel about Rusty the Rooster?

LIBRARIAN: I've never seen Rusty before.

ASSISTANT: You don't attend the County Fair?

LIBRARIAN: No. I wish the people of Tinytown would visit the library more than the County Fair.

(Detective holds up the torn encyclopedia page from the barn.)

DETECTIVE: Have you ever seen this piece of paper?

LIBRARIAN: It looks like someone tore a page out of one of my books, an encyclopedia. *(Inspects the page.)* Look! There is a sentence that is underlined, "The average life span of a rooster is 10 to 12 years."

(Librarian grabs the encyclopedia and opens it up to reveal the torn page.)

ASSISTANT: Who was the last person to check this book out?

(Librarian flips to the front cover. She gasps.)

DETECTIVE: What!? Who is it?

LIBRARIAN: It's…it's…Danny Brown!

(The Detective, Assistant and Librarian exit. The Brown Family enters with Ron and Farm Worker.)

SALLY: What are we going to do? Rusty's competition is in one hour!

MRS. BROWN: Don't worry, dear. We need to trust the detectives.

(Detective and Assistant enter.)

FARM WORKER: Any news about Rusty?

DETECTIVE: We have a main suspect.

RON THE ROOSTER TRAINER: Who?

ASSISTANT: Danny Brown!

ALL EXCEPT DANNY: Danny?!?!

DETECTIVE: Danny, did you take Rusty?

DANNY: YES, I did.

MRS. BROWN: Why?

DANNY: I found out at the library that roosters only live for about ten years. I was worried that you were going to turn Rusty into chicken soup after this competition. He doesn't deserve to get eaten!

MR. BROWN: Danny, we would never do that.

DANNY: Really?

MRS. BROWN: He's a part of our family.

DANNY: I'll go get him—he's in my room!

(Danny returns with Rusty. Rusty enters eating a carrot.)

RUSTY: Hey, everyone.

ALL: Rusty!

DANNY: We better get to that competition!

(All exit. County Fair Judge enters with Mrs. Eviction, Jenny, Jasper, Hattie and the Rooster Rooters.)

COUNTY FAIR JUDGE: Well, I guess if we don't have any other competitors, I will have to announce the winner. The first-place winner is…

SALLY: Wait! Rusty's here!

(Everyone enters. Rusty does his cool trick perfectly.)

COUNTY FAIR JUDGE: And the first-place prize goes to…Rusty the Rooster for the eleventh time!

(Everyone cheers.)

DETECTIVE: And that is how we solved this story.

ASSISTANT: Very true.

DETECTIVE: Case closed!

(End of play.)

The Author Speaks

What inspired you to write this play?

My initial motivation to write **The Case of the Missing Rooster** was very practical. I was teaching a class of students and we needed to have a short performance at the end of the semester. Out of this necessity grew an idea for a short play in a mystery style. As the characters and world began to develop, I wanted to ensure that all of my students had a moment to shine, that the play was humorous and engaging, and that the script was action-oriented and character rich.

Was the structure or other elements of the play influenced by any other work?

I love mystery and detective stories! In addition to watching detective movies, I even remember writing a short detective play with my sister and my cousins when we were kids. However, this is my first comedic mystery story as an adult playwright.

Have you dealt with the same theme in other works that you have written?

I also wrote a ten-minute play for the middle school students at my current school. That mystery was about a mascot missing from the school. It was similarly a balance of detective-style tropes mixed in with my sense of humor and goofy dialogue.

What writers have had the most profound effect on your style?

Although I have a clear voice of my own as a playwright, I've been inspired by many playwrights who write specifically for young audiences: Suzan Zeder, Y York, Barry Kornhauser, Laurie Brooks, Dwayne Hartford, Miriam Gonzales, just to name a few. I've studied and/or met many of these people through their plays, development workshops, conferences, etc., and many other playwrights for young audiences have not only been an example to me of great writing, but have provided support, encouragement, and mentorship over the years.

What do you hope to achieve with this work?
I hope that *The Case of the Missing Rooster* finds a place in upper elementary and middle school classrooms. When younger students study plays in school, they are often plays written to impart certain facts or vocabulary. These "educational" scripts are often inactive and have lengthy paragraphs/monologues that are not very exciting to perform. Hopefully, my play will be accessible to classroom teachers and engaging for students to perform.

What were the biggest challenges involved in the writing of this play?
When I first wrote this play, the biggest challenges were trying to write enough characters into a short play for every student in my class. Not only that, but they also needed to be substantial characters that had some development through the story. Also, I remember writing this play during a winter break that I had, so I only had a couple weeks to write it and have it ready for rehearsals with my students.

What are the most common mistakes that occur in productions of your work?
When I see a production that is very different from the vision I had in my mind, I don't usually see it as a mistake. If the director/cast interpreted something in a way that I didn't expect or don't find true or accurate, I usually take this as a sign to interrogate my own writing to see how I could have conveyed my intent more precisely. Sometimes there are productions that have performers with varying skill levels. As a drama teacher, I often attribute mistakes or poor choices to the learning process.

What inspired you to become a playwright?

As a child, I loved reading and stories! My parents often took me and my sisters to see plays. So, I know the seeds of my playwriting life were planted from a very young age. During my undergraduate studies at Ripon College, I took a Children's Theater class. A few of the assignments included adapting and writing children's plays. I loved it! I also had a chance to perform the role of Stuart Little in Joseph Robinette's *Stuart Little*. As a performer, I got to see how engaged young audiences could be. All of these interests converged at Arizona State University during my master's degree studies, when I began writing plays for the first time.

How did you research the subject?

I did not do any research for this play. In lieu of research, I was able to tap into my collective ideas about detective stories and tropes and apply those to this imaginative piece. For other plays I've written, research has been a very important component. This changes from project to project.

Are any characters modeled after real life or historical figures?

Not in particular. In terms of the Detective and the Detective's Assistant, I've been influenced by popular detective characters/stories from my youth: Veronica Mars, Agatha Christie, Jessica Fletcher, Nancy Drew, Sherlock Holmes, Inspector Gadget, etc. However, the characters from *The Case of the Missing Rooster* are not directly modeled after any specific character.

What is your writing process?

My writing process varies from project to project. I'm very good with deadlines, so if I have the good fortune of working on a deadline, then I will parse out my time leading up to the deadline and work in two to three-hour chunks. I have a full-time job as a public school Drama Specialist, so I often have to carve out little chunks of time to write: weekends, holidays, summer break. I wish I had the discipline to write every day, but alas, I find ways to be productive and creative with the time I have.

Shakespeare gave advice to the players in *Hamlet*; if you could give advice to your cast what would it be?
Have fun and embrace the characters! Even though this is a short play and you may only have a few lines, challenge yourself to make your character memorable through your dialogue, action, gestures, facial expressions, vocal variety and connection with your fellow performers.

About the Author

Anne Negri is a K-8 Drama Specialist in the Evanston/Skokie District 65 public schools of Illinois. She is a graduate of Arizona State University's MFA program in theatre for youth. She earned her BA in Theatre, French, and K-12 education from Ripon College in Ripon, Wisconsin. Her play, **With Two Wings**, published by Dramatic Publishing, received an American Alliance for Theatre and Education Distinguished Play Award, a Kennedy Center ACTF Theatre for Youth Audiences Award, was a finalist in the Bonderman Playwriting for Youth Symposium, and has been produced nationally (Childsplay, Northwestern University, The Growing Stage) and internationally (Theatre Ma, Japan, National University of Tainan, Taiwan). Other plays that have received productions / tours / workshops / development include: ***Girls Who Wear Glasses, Cave Boys, The JunGirl Book, Maddi's Fridge, Not a Test*** and ***The Dancing Dog!***

GOGGLES
by Nicole B. Adkins

CAST OF CHARACTERS

KELLEN, 5th grade girl, misses Skyler. Her brother is driving her crazy.

CAMERON, in-between 1st-3rd grade, Kellen's brother, loves skateboarding, really wants his big sister's attention.

SKYLER, 5th grade girl, used to be Kellen's best friend but has rather disappeared since she got Mega Game Goggles and started hanging with Georgie.

GEORGIE, 5th grade girl, Skyler's friend, really into the Goggles. She and Kellen don't really like each other.

MGG (MEGA GAME GUIDE), 1-3+ people, a digital being/beings. The Mega Goggles guide/chorus could be played by multiple actors saying the lines in unison, or the lines could be alternated, or one actor could say the lines while the other actors helped to create the world. These actors could double as partygoers in Kellen's Mega Game World experience.

Genders may be switched as needed. If genders are changed, pronouns, related nouns, etc, may be changed accordingly.

PRODUCTION NOTES

Goggles may look however the production team wishes. They could be as simple as painted swim goggles (the big kind that go partially over the nose would probably look best) or glasses with painted cardboard additions glued to them...whatever you can dream up.

Though the play could still be produced effectively without

these elements, if the production team has access to a projector and screen, these could be used to help create Kellen and Cameron's house/front porch, and then to bring Mega Game World to life. For example, when Kellen appears there, we could see an image/video of a colorful, abstract, digital world behind her, and later we could see things/places she requests (the car/motorcycle/etc., the beach, a disco ball/party setting, etc.).

(Lights up on KELLEN, grade 5, sitting on her front porch, texting. Her brother CAMERON, younger, is playing around on his skateboard.)

CAMERON: Kel! Watch!

KELLEN: Busy.

CAMERON: I wanna go to the skatepark.

KELLEN: Not right now! Told you, Skyler's coming over... *(Gets a text.)* Hey — she says she has a surprise for me.

CAMERON: Then can we go? Mom said we could go!

KELLEN: Depends on what Skyler wants to do... Wonder what the surprise is.

CAMERON: I thought you guys weren't even friends anymore.

KELLEN: What?!

CAMERON: Last week when she invited Georgie over and not you and they went to that Goggle tournament thing you said —

KELLEN: Don't you dare tell her that.

CAMERON: *Well,* if you take me to the skatepark...

KELLEN: If you tell her I will make you eat your skateboard.

CAMERON: She won't wanna go. She used to be fun. But now all she does is sit around wearing those Goggles. It's dumb.

KELLEN: You're just jealous Mom won't let you have a pair.

CAMERON: So are you.

(Kellen stands to look for Skyler. Cameron starts to skate off.)

KELLEN: MOM SAID STAY IN THE DRIVEWAY UNLESS I'M WITH YOU!

(Cameron sighs and comes back. SKYLER, grade 5 and GEORGIE, her friend, enter. They are both carrying Mega Game Goggles, which are awesome. Better than awesome. Skyler hides a bag behind her back.)

CAMERON: *(Does Skateboard trick.)* Hey Skyler! Watch this!

SKYLER: Nice, Cam! Hey Kellen!

KELLEN: Skyler!! Georgie...didn't know you were coming...

GEORGIE: Spent the night last night.

KELLEN: Oh...

CAMERON: Wanna go to the skatepark with us?

SKYLER: Maybe later. I would've invited you last night too, Kel, but we were Goggling. I knew you'd be bored. But then... this morning something *amazing* happened, the best thing EVER—and I have the hugest surprise for you!!!

GEORGIE: Give them to her so we can go already.

KELLEN: Give me what?

GEORGIE: Going to Goggle, K?

(Georgie sits; puts on her Goggles. She trances out.)

SKYLER: *(Smiles mysteriously.)* Wait'll you see... Close your eyes and hold out your hands.

(Kellen does.)

Don't peek!

(Skyler puts the bag in Kellen's hands.)

Happy early birthday!!!

(Kellen pulls Mega Game Goggles out of the bag.)

KELLEN: OH. MY. WOW! Seriously?!!

CAMERON: Mom's never going to let you keep those.

KELLEN: Stuff it, Cam.

CAMERON: She says they're too expensive, and she read a bunch of articles that said —

KELLEN: Yeah I know what she read but she doesn't have to pay for them and she can't say no to a present! Thank you, SKYLER! But — how??

SKYLER: My dad surprised me with the Deluxe Goggles this morning!! Faster processing, better graphics, more levels — but the old ones are still super cool...just wait. I know we haven't been hanging out a lot lately...but now with the extra pair, I thought maybe...

KELLEN: *(Touched:)* Thanks, Sky.

CAMERON: Mom says those things turn your brain into space jelly and your butt [bum] into a pancake. They'll probably turn you boring, just like —

KELLEN: CAMERON! Sorry. He's so *dumb* sometimes!

CAMERON: Am not!

SKYLER: Haha, no worries. I get it. My baby sister is the same way.

CAMERON: I'm not a baby! And I'm not dumb!

SKYLER: Sorry, didn't mean it that way, Cam. Now, Kel — TRY them. Come on!

(Skyler puts on her Goggles, sits and trances out.)

CAMERON: Let me try.

KELLEN: No way. *I* haven't even tried them yet... *(Squeals.)* And they're *mine!*

(Kellen looks at the Goggles, then at Skyler. She puts them on. Music. Maybe the lights change. Skyler, Georgie and Cameron all exit instantly. We are in Mega Game World. MEGA GAME

GUIDE (MGG), a genie or wizard-like being (could be played by multiple actors), appears. MGG takes off Kellen's Goggles. Kellen stands, looking around.)

MGG: Welcome, Initiate, to Mega Game World, where all your dreams come true...

KELLEN: Wow... This is AMAZING! Where am I? It feels so real...

(MGG puts her/his hands on Kellen's head.)

Whoa! Hello...

MGG: Please stand by for a mind-scan...

(We hear a machine-like whir, then a beep like a microwave alarm.)

Please state your wishes, Kellen. We are here to serve.

KELLEN: You know my name!!

MGG: What do you wish for, Kellen? Anything you want is yours.

KELLEN: *(Jumping up and down, squealing:)* Whoa! Ok... Um... Maybe...I wish I knew how to drive and had a car?

(We hear a car beep. MGG gives car keys to Kellen. Kellen looks out and squeals.)

How did you know my favorite color is red?!! OK, what about a — motorcycle?

(Smaller beep, MGG gives her more keys.)

A boat!

(A beep, more keys.)

An airplane!

(Sound of an airplane landing, more keys).

A never-ending chocolate bar!!

(MGG gives her a huge chocolate bar.)

KELLEN: *(Takes a bite.)* Um...tastes less...chocolatey than I'd imagined... Kinda tastes like nothing.

MGG: If you'd like to order the Mega Deluxe Goggles with a full sensory panel, please insert credit card.

KELLEN: No, it's fine.

(Kellen hands MGG back the chocolate bar.)

I wish...I was at the beach?

(We hear waves and seagulls. Maybe it gets brighter. MGG brings in a reclining beach chair. Kellen looks around, amazed. She sits in the beach chair.)

Awesome. *(Squinting:)* Can I have Kay Ray sunglasses, please?

(MGG gives her the sunglasses. She puts them on.)

(Laughing:) A kazoo?

(MGG hands it to her, she toots it a bit then gives it back.)

The newest Sarah Signa book!

(MGG hands her a book. She opens it.)

Blank inside?

MGG: For full text, please insert credit card.

KELLEN: Um—no thanks, er, never mind...

(She gives the empty book back.)

What about...can I swim here?

MGG: For full aquatic sensory experience, please insert credit card.

KELLEN: Never mind...

MGG: What do you wish for most, Kellen?

KELLEN: I guess...I wish Skyler was here with me?

(We hear a whirring noise.)

MGG: Scanning memory bank and local devices... User currently occupied. Do Not Disturb mode.

KELLEN: But I thought this was something we were supposed to do together...

MGG: Sending proxy.

(Skyler enters, zombie-like.)

KELLEN: Hi Skyler!

SKYLER: *(Empty, brainwashed voice:)* Hi, bestie.

(Kellen waves her hands in front of Skyler's face; Skyler's expression remains unchanged.)

KELLEN: Thanks... Um, what now? What should we do next?

MGG: Turning on Wish Anticipation Mode.

(Whirring noise.)

SKYLER: How about a party?

(Dance music. Maybe disco lights. Georgie enters. Georgie and Skyler dance and laugh in a fake, hollow way [more actors could join in if you have them]. They keep dancing through the following sequence:)

Come on, Kellen! Dance with us!

GEORGIE: *(Empty, brainwashed voice:)* Totally! I'm so sorry I've never noticed how cool you are before. Let's dance!

(Kellen dances halfheartedly. Cameron enters, skating around Kellen.)

CAMERON: Hey sis! What're you doing? Can I play too? Can I?

KELLEN: What are you doing here?? I didn't wish for you! Get lost!

MGG: Our apologies. Recalibrating.

(We hear a whirring noise. MGG removes Cameron.)

CAMERON: Hellllp!!! *(Off:)* Sis! Sis! Heeeeellllp! Where am I? It's getting dark...

KELLEN: *(A little worried:)* Cameron?

CAMERON: *(Trails off:)* Keelllleennnn...

(The music gets louder. Georgie and Skyler dance closer and closer to her. While they are dancing, they acquire "pancake butts.")

SKYLER & GEORGIE: *(Empty, brainwashed voices and fake laughter:)* Come on, Kellen, dance with us!

(The music gets louder, they get closer. Kellen is unsettled.)

KELLEN: Skyler? Georgie? *(Points to their rear ends:)* What's up with your...?

SKYLER & GEORGIE: What do you mean, Kellen?

KELLEN: Why do you both sound so weird?

SKYLER & GEORGIE: What do you mean, Kellen?

SKYLER: Everything is wonderful.

GEORGIE: Isn't it wonderful here?

SKYLER & GEORGIE: *(Singing like a commercial:)* Mega Game Goggles!

(They advance, Zombie-like, toward her.)

KELLEN: Cameron!

(No answer.)

Have you guys seen my brother?

SKYLER: Who?

GEORGIE: You don't have a brother, Kellen.

SKYLER & GEORGIE: You never had a brother.

(They move closer and closer. They pull out a third pancake butt.)

KELLEN: You guys are freaking me out... I don't want a pancake butt [bum]! CAMERON!

SKYLER & GEORGIE: Don't you want to experience the next level, Kel?

GEORGIE: Don't you want to be one of us?

SKYLER: Don't you want to be best friends again?

KELLEN: Yeah! I mean, I do—I did, but this is all fake! And I feel like I don't even really know you anymore—

SKYLER: You can, though! You only have to -

(They corner her with the pancake butt.)

SKYLER & GEORGIE: Join us, Kellen! Join our world...

(They come closer.)

KELLEN: Stop it!

MGG: What do you *want most*, Kellen? Whatever you wish is yours...

(Skyler and George reach out like hungry zombies. They are about to grab her —)

KELLEN: Get me OUT OF HERE!

MGG: As you wish. Disengaging. Goodbye, Kellen.

(The music ends as MGG disappears, taking the jacket, the kazoo, the keys, pancake butt, etc. Skyler and Georgie are back on the porch wearing their goggles. Kellen's goggles are back on. She takes them off. She looks around, groggy. She gets up. Cameron is nowhere to be seen.)

KELLEN: ...Cameron? CAMERON! Oh no, no, no, no, no... Skyler! Skyler?! Georgie?

(She shakes Skyler and Georgie. They are unresponsive.)

My brother—he's not here—help! I think something happened to him! Cameron! Where are you?? Mom's going to freak... Cameron! Where are you? CAMERON!

(Cameron skates in. Kellen hugs him, hard.)

CAMERON: I'm right here! Sorry—

KELLEN: WHERE WERE YOU?! I thought someone took you or something!

CAMERON: Just skating around the cul-de-sac—

KELLEN: Mom said—

CAMERON: I know! But I tried to ask you! You wouldn't answer or even move. It was weird.

KELLEN: You scared me! Don't leave the driveway without me or Mom!!

CAMERON: You scared me too.

KELLEN: *(Beat.)* I'm sorry.

CAMERON: Me too. So can we go to the skatepark now?

KELLEN: *(Laughs a little.)* Hold on a sec, OK? *(Tries to get Skyler's attention:)* Skyler, hey!

(Skyler is unresponsive. Finally, Kellen puts the Goggles back in the bag, placing it next to Skyler. She writes a text. Cameron reads over her shoulder. Kellen lets him.)

CAMERON: *(Reading:)* "Call me if you want a break from the Goggles." Really?

KELLEN: You wanna go to the skatepark now, or what?

CAMERON: YES!

KELLEN: OK. Well, um... Bye, Skyler... Georgie.

(They are unresponsive.)

CAMERON: So weird.

KELLEN: Come on. Let's go.

CAMERON: Thanks for taking me. *(As they are exiting:)* Hey! Wait'll you see my kickflip! I've been working on it, and I'm getting really good!

KELLEN: I bet.

CAMERON: So what were the goggles like anyway?

KELLEN: Oh, boy. Well...

(They keep chatting together as they exit. After a moment, Skyler takes off her headset.)

SKYLER: Guys!! You wouldn't believe it! I just unlocked a new level! It's amazing!!

(No one answers.)

Kellen?

(She looks around. Kellen is gone.)

Georgie?

(Georgie is unresponsive. After a moment, Skyler shrugs and puts her Goggles back on.)

(End of play.)

The Author Speaks

What inspired you to write this play?
I wanted to explore technology addiction and how tech has the power to shape and affect our interpersonal relationships. I wondered what might happen between characters whose use of it and exposure to it differs. What happens when you are the person left behind by the latest tech craze, and ultimately, is that a good thing or a bad thing, or maybe something in-between?

Was the structure or other elements of the play influenced by any other work?
I like science fiction quite a bit and am fascinated by imagined worlds, so while I can't think of any specific influences for this piece, I do suspect that elements from sci-fi I've seen/read frequently thread themselves into my work.

Have you dealt with the same theme in other works that you have written?
I often write about characters who are deciding who they are and who they want to become. Kellen, the protagonist of this play, is no exception. She has to choose whether it's worth it to lose herself in the glitter of an imagined world, or if reality (maybe without her best friend) is where she truly fits.

What writers have had the most profound effect on your style?
I have always been a voracious reader. As a kid, I spent years reading all the myths, legends and original fairy tales I could find. I moved from there to authors who explore the mythic and fantastical in their writing (often fantasy or sci-fi), such as George MacDonald, Hans Christian Andersen, Ursula K. Le Guin, Madeleine L'Engle, C.S. Lewis, Lois Lowry and Ray Bradbury. I also loved authors of classic books with strong female characters, such as Jane Austen and L.M. Montgomery.

My years working as an actor in theatre for young audiences were also deeply formative; I was amazed to discover the work of playwrights like Suzan Zeder and José Cruz González and to get to perform in scripts like **The Yellow Boat** by David Saar. For the past few years, I've been especially enamored by the research, experimentation and focus on audience inclusion in TVY (Theatre for the Very Young). I have long been a devourer of books and plays and find that I nearly always have something to learn from other writers, artists and audiences.

What do you hope to achieve with this work?
I hope that students performing in and seeing this play will be inspired to question and talk about the role of technology in all our lives. I'd love, specifically, to spark discussion about how technology affects our interpersonal relationships. How can it connect or alienate us? Today's students will be affected by and may have a hand in the future evolution of this ever-changing field. Dreaming now about what technology should look like or offer in the future could end up providing important balance. If this play can further that exploration, I'll be delighted.

What were the biggest challenges involved in the writing of this play?
Landing on the right structure was the greatest challenge. This play deals with several themes, including sibling relationships, fading friendships, addiction and the lure of shiny things, all in the space of 12-15 minutes. I wanted all of these themes to reflect and inform each other. Finding a way to do this without the script feeling overburdened was a journey.

What are the most common mistakes that occur in productions of your work?
I don't know that I would call any exploration a *mistake* (unless someone changes the text without permission). Some ideas

and experiments play better than others, but particularly in an educational environment, that's part of the joy of the process! This said, I would encourage producing teams to do your table work. Talk about and discuss the characters, their world and their motivations—before and during the process of putting the play on its feet. I often find that there is a correlation between the success of a production and the amount of time that the director has built into the rehearsal process for the team to dive into and explore the world of the play.

What inspired you to become a playwright?
My father had his undergraduate degree in theatre and owned a video production company through my childhood. My mother was always a poet and a writer, and ran the production company with my dad, writing many of the scripts for commercials, how-to videos and other jobs. Subsequently I spent a lot of time on set, either just hanging around or being thrown into projects as a handy, free actor. I participated in theatre also from a very early age. (My first appearance on stage was as the dove in **Godspell**...if you know the show, there is no dove. I spent most of the show scratching my tights). Anyway, I was bitten by that infamous theatre bug! I acted, consumed theatre, read every book I could find and wrote stories and plays from a very early age. Given the combination of my parents' talents, my great respect for both of them and my love of theatre and literature, being a playwright kind of felt inevitable. Also, though I began as an actor and that influences every play I write, I became far more entranced by creating and peopling entire worlds than actually being onstage myself. I love to try and create worlds and characters that actors, designers and directors might enjoy bringing to life, and to see what new colors and depth they bring to my initial vision.

What is your writing process?

Every play is its own creature, and thereby demands a slightly different process. That said, I do have a general method. Usually, first I get the idea/image, and then I spend some time rolling it around and shaping it my mind, teasing it into the semblance of a story. I go on walks, do dishes, shower, all while thinking about this new world of my imagining (and muttering to myself, I'll admit). Then, generally, I write a treatment—kind of like an outline, but with a wider focus (leaving room to jot down thoughts about theme, visual/music-related inspiration, character descriptions, etc.) in a "presentable" fashion—something I could share with potential collaborators for the purposes of brainstorming. I challenge myself to keep it to 1-2 pages. Sometimes I use the wonderful "Tarot" exercise from Suzan Zeder's book *Spaces of Creation*, involving index cards. It is an amazing help in structuring a play and in ensuring that your story has the right amount of tension. Then, I try to find a good chunk of time to pour out the first draft, like water, without letting myself get in my own way or in the way of the characters that are emerging. Then I put the script away for a day or two. Then I read it, do rewrites, put it away, read it, and so on, as long as necessary, until I'm ready to share it with trusted readers (usually my mom and husband). Next, I find actors to help me hear it aloud. Then a whole new process begins! Hearing a play aloud and inviting in collaborators can really reshape a play. In 1889, playwright and actor Steele MacKaye said, "Plays are not written—they are rewritten." I am a firm believer in this idea. VERY occasionally for me a play has seemed to "write itself" and has stayed relatively intact from the first draft to the end, but that is *definitely* the exception rather than the rule, and I have learned to really embrace the rewriting process. It gives me the opportunity to play with and explore the imagined world and its denizens!

Shakespeare gave advice to the players in *Hamlet*; if you could give advice to your cast what would it be?
Figure out what the characters want more than anything. Find and explore the different ways they go about getting what they want. Be fearless and generous!

About the Author

Nicole B. Adkins has taught classes and workshops to students of various ages at theatres, K-12 schools and universities. Her plays have been performed at Children's Theatre of Charlotte, Hollins University, Mill Mountain Theatre, Studio Roanoke, Creative Drama Children's Theatre in Winston-Salem, NC, SkyPilot Theatre in Los Angeles, the American International School in Guanghzou China and other theatres, schools and museums nationally and abroad. She has six plays published through YouthPLAYS, where she also serves as Artistic Associate. She collaborated with Matt Omasta of Utah State University on a book entitled *Playwriting and Young Audiences: Collected Wisdom and Practical Advice from the Field* (Intellect Press, 2017). National playwriting awards include the Waldo M. and Grace C. Bonderman Award and recognition in the Beverly Hills Theatre Guild Marilyn Hall competition. A Hollins Children's Literature MFA graduate and Playwright's Lab Core Faculty member, Nicole is also a member of Dramatists Guild and TYA/USA. Website: www.nicolebadkins.com.

FRANKIE GETS IT RIGHT
by Matt Buchanan

CAST OF CHARACTERS

FRANKIE, any gender, eight or nine. Eager and helpful but forgetful.

MOM, female (but Mom could easily be Dad—no line changes needed). Kind, patient, and harassed.

JODY, any gender, around eight or nine.

PARKER, any gender, around eight or nine.

CORY, any gender, around eight or nine.

NEW PARENT (mother or father). Proud but exhausted.

SHOPKEEPER, any gender. Brisk and friendly.

MAIL CARRIER, any gender. Not too bright.

Various CIRCUS PERFORMERS, all genders.

GROCER, any gender. Jovial and bright.

SETTING

A city or downtown neighborhood in an unspecified time and location. The idea is that Frankie walks from home to the market and back, encountering various people and situations along the way and passing the same locations on the way home. This can be accomplished in a number of ways. If your space is small and there is easy passage from left to right backstage, Frankie could cross the stage from right to left again and again, running around backstage in between, so that Frankie's direction of travel is consistent until arrival at the market. The process could be reversed on the way home. Individual scenes along the way could be set up as Frankie is crossing backstage. If this is not possible, Frankie could cross from right to left, then from left to right, etc., and allow the context to make clear that Frankie is traveling in a straight line from home to the market. Again, each scene would be set up as Frankie is backstage. If the stage is very large, another possibility would be to have all of the scenes set up at once across the stage, so that the stage represents the entirety of the distance from home to the market (though be sure to use lighting to focus on the relevant scene so that the others don't distract from the story). You will no doubt think of other creative ways to address the problem as well.

(Frankie's house. MOM stands center stage, holding a grocery list and looking a little exasperated.)

MOM: *(Calling:)* Frankie! *(Louder:)* Frankie!

(Noises off. Running feet, several crashes, as of falling dishes or furniture. FRANKIE enters at a run and stands respectfully before Mom.)

Frankie, there you are. I was afraid you'd fallen down the sink. Now listen. I need you to go to the market for me. Do you think you can do that?

(Frankie nods enthusiastically.)

Are you sure, dear? You know how forgetful you are.

(Frankie shrugs.)

You know you are, dear. Remember when I asked you to go next door and borrow a cup of sugar?

(Frankie nods.)

Do you remember what you came home with?

(Frankie gives a negative head shake.)

You came home with a box of sink washers, five bottles of balsamic vinegar, and a Cavalier King Charles Spaniel.

(Frankie shrugs.)

Do you think you can remember better this time?

(Frankie nods enthusiastically.)

Now listen closely. Here's what I need you to buy: A dozen eggs…

FRANKIE: *(Repeating as a memory aid:)* A dozen eggs.

MOM: A pound of butter…

FRANKIE: A pound of butter. A dozen eggs and a pound of butter.

MOM: And two pints of milk.

FRANKIE: Two pints of milk. A dozen eggs, a pound of butter, and two pints of milk.

MOM: That's right, dear.

FRANKIE: A dozen eggs, a pound of butter, and two pints of milk.

MOM: Here's some money.

(Mom hands Frankie some money, which Frankie pockets.)

FRANKIE: A dozen eggs, a pound of butter, and two pints of milk.

MOM: If there's any change left over, you may have ONE…

(She holds up one finger.)

…piece of candy.

FRANKIE: One piece of candy. A dozen eggs, a pound of butter, and two pints of milk. And one piece of candy.

MOM: Now hurry along, dear. I want to make a very special cake, and I need those groceries. Hurry along.

FRANKIE: One piece of candy. A dozen eggs, a pound of butter, and two pints of milk. And one piece of candy.

(Frankie "leaves" the house and sets off for the market. As Mom exits, JODY, PARKER, and CORY appear, playing with a jump rope. Parker and Cory spin the rope as Jody jumps. Frankie approaches them.)

JODY: Hi, Frankie!

FRANKIE: A dozen eggs, a pound of butter, and two pints of milk.

JODY: That's great, Frankie. Hey, if you're not in a hurry, can you help us play? We're trying for a new record.

PARKER: You hold the rope, so I can jump.

(Frankie takes the rope from Parker.)

FRANKIE: And one piece of candy.

PARKER: Thanks, Frankie!

(As Frankie and Cory spin the rope, Parker and Jody jump. Jody chants.)

JODY: PARKER AND JODY WENT TO THE SHORE.
PICKING UP SEASHELLS FROM THE SEA FLOOR.
RED ONES, YELLOW ONES, COLORS GALORE.
HOW MANY SEASHELLS WERE ON THAT SHORE?
ONE!
TWO!
THREE!
FOUR!
FIVE!
SIX!
SEVEN!
EIGHT!
NINE!

(Parker stumbles.)

PARKER: *(Disappointed:)* Nine. Awwww.

CORY: Nine's not bad. Nine's pretty good. Right, Frankie?

(Frankie nods and hands the rope back to Parker.)

FRANKIE: Nine.

PARKER: Thanks, Frankie. So long!

(Frankie continues on the way to the market.)

FRANKIE: *(Happily:)* Nine!

(As the children exit, a NEW PARENT [mother or father] appears with a baby carriage. S/he is rather frantically wheeling the carriage back and forth. A bench also appears.)

NEW PARENT: Oh, hello, Frankie! How nice to see you!

FRANKIE: Nine dozen eggs, a pound of butter, and two pints of milk.

NEW PARENT: My goodness! That's a lot of eggs!

FRANKIE: And one piece of candy.

NEW PARENT: Uh huh. Say, Frankie, if you're not in a hurry, would you mind pushing little Skipper around for a while? She cries every time I stop, and I really need to sit down.

(Frankie shrugs amiably and begins pushing the carriage back and forth. The New Parent sits on the bench and rubs sore feet.)

My goodness, that feels good. You have no idea how much work a baby is, Frankie. She's our first, you know. And she's growing so fast.

(Frankie nods politely.)

Why, my goodness, would you believe it—she's already eighteen pounds!

FRANKIE: Eighteen pounds?

NEW PARENT: Eighteen pounds. Imagine! *(Proudly:)* Doctor says that's just where she ought to be.

FRANKIE: *(Happily:)* Eighteen pounds.

NEW PARENT: My goodness, she's just perfect. Well, Frankie, I think I can take over now.

(S/he does.)

Thanks so much, Frankie! You have a lovely day.

(Frankie continues on the way to the market.)

FRANKIE: *(Happily:)* Eighteen pounds!

(As the New Parent exits, a SHOPKEEPER appears [perhaps in coveralls with the name of a hardware store on them] with a stepladder and some tools.)

SHOPKEEPER: Well, well, well. Hello, young Frankie!

FRANKIE: Nine dozen eggs, eighteen pounds of butter, and two pints of milk.

SHOPKEEPER: Is that so? Well, well, well. That's a lot of butter.

FRANKIE: And one piece of candy.

SHOPKEEPER: Well, well, well. Say, listen, Frankie. If you're not in a hurry, how about holding the ladder for me?

(Frankie shrugs amiably and holds the ladder. The Shopkeeper starts up it.)

Got to get this sign up. We're running a special sale on barrels.

FRANKIE: Barrels?

(The Shopkeeper begins to nail up the sign. [Note: if you want, you can fly something in so that the Shopkeeper can actually nail a real sign to something, but it's perfectly okay to mime the sign. A hammer, and maybe a sound effect of hammering – which could be made by the actor tapping a foot or by another performer offstage – are plenty to get the idea across.])

SHOPKEEPER: Yep. Never know when you're going to need a nice barrel. We got a special deal on barrels – this week only.

FRANKIE: Barrels.

SHOPKEEPER: That's right. There now… *(Surveying the sign:)* That looks just about right.

(The Shopkeeper descends the ladder.)

Thanks very much, young Frankie. You have yourself a wonderful day!

> *(Frankie continues on the way to the market.)*

FRANKIE: *(Happily:)* Barrels!

> *(As the Shopkeeper exits, a MAIL CARRIER appears, dragging a heavy mailbag and looking with puzzlement at a letter.)*

MAIL CARRIER: Howdy, Frankie.

FRANKIE: Nine dozen eggs, eighteen pounds of butter, and two barrels of milk.

MAIL CARRIER: You don't say! Son of a gun! That's a lot of milk! You'll need a lot of cookies for that, I'll bet.

FRANKIE: And one piece of candy.

MAIL CARRIER: Sure, or candy if you prefer. Hey pal, maybe you can help me out here, if you're not in a hurry.

> *(Frankie shrugs amiably.)*

See, I've got this letter, and I don't know where it goes. Says number thirty-one.

FRANKIE: Thirty-one?

MAIL CARRIER: Thirty-one. And I know where number thirty is—it's right there. *(Points.)* And number thirty-two is that big house. *(Points.)* But son of a gun, I don't know where thirty-one is.

FRANKIE: *(Determined:)* Thirty-one.

> *(Frankie conducts a thorough search of the neighborhood, looking for number thirty-one. Eventually he finds it, right in the middle of the stage. [Note: there is no need for physical houses or stoops. This can all be mimed.] Frankie points triumphantly.)*

Thirty-one!

(The Mail Carrier squints at the "house number," then at the letter.)

MAIL CARRIER: Thirty-one! Son of a gun! And it's right between twenty-nine and thirty-three. That's a big coincidence. Good job! I woulda never found it. Thanks, Frankie! Have a good one!

(Frankie continues on the way to the market.)

FRANKIE: *(Happily:)* Thirty-one!

(As the Mail Carrier exits, the strains of "Entry of the Gladiators" [or other appropriate circus music] are heard. A whole troupe of CIRCUS PERFORMERS crosses the stage in front of Frankie, going the opposite direction. Several of them juggle eggs [if you have anyone who can really juggle] or carry stacks of egg cartons. One pulls a wagon loaded down with boxes labeled "Butter." Two more roll large barrels labeled "Milk." None of them seems to notice Frankie, who watches, transfixed, as they pass by and off. Frankie looks after them for a second, then shrugs and continues the journey to the market. The GROCER enters, perhaps wheeling a counter with a cash register, etc. Frankie approaches the counter.)

GROCER: Well now, hello, Frankie! And what can I do for you this fine day?

(Frankie takes a deep breath. Big moment.)

FRANKIE: Nine dozen eggs, eighteen pounds of butter, and two barrels of milk, please.

GROCER: Great Scott!

FRANKIE: And thirty-one pieces of candy!

GROCER: Thirty-one!?

FRANKIE: Please.

GROCER: *(Sadly:)* Well now, Frankie, I hate to disappoint you. I surely do. But you see, the circus is in town, and they pretty much cleaned me out. I simply don't have nine dozen eggs.

(The Grocer looks for eggs — perhaps under the counter or on a shelf behind it. [This can be mimed.])

In fact, all I have is eleven. No, wait…twelve. Twelve eggs. Will that do?

FRANKIE: Twelve eggs?

GROCER: That's an even dozen.

FRANKIE: A dozen eggs?

(Frankie shrugs accommodatingly.)

GROCER: Well now, that's fine. Here they are.

(The Grocer puts the eggs on the counter.)

Now, butter. Let me see.

FRANKIE: Eighteen pounds of butter.

GROCER: Yes.

FRANKIE: Please.

GROCER: Well, now, those circus folk sure do love their butter. All I have left *(Looking for the butter:)* …is sixteen ounces. Will that do?

FRANKIE: Sixteen ounces of butter?

GROCER: That comes to exactly one pound.

FRANKIE: A pound of butter? And a dozen eggs?

(Frankie shrugs accommodatingly.)

GROCER: Well now, that's fine. Here it is.

(The Grocer puts the butter on the counter.)

And milk, did you say?

FRANKIE: Two barrels of milk, please.

GROCER: Well, now I don't know what those circus folk needed so much milk for. Do tigers drink milk? But they sure cleaned me out. Even took the barrels. All I've got left is one quart.

FRANKIE: One quart of milk?

GROCER: That's right. Two pints, to be exact.

FRANKIE: Two pints of milk? And a pound of butter and a dozen eggs?

(*Frankie shrugs accommodatingly.*)

GROCER: Well now, that's fine. Here it is.

(*The Grocer puts two pint bottles of milk on the counter.*)

Shall I put it all in a bag for you?

(*The Grocer puts the food in a bag. Frankie pulls money from a pocket and shyly hands it to the Grocer. The Grocer rings up the sale on the cash register.*)

Well now, let's see. That's a dozen eggs, a pound of butter, and two pints of milk. Well now, Frankie…there's just a little left over. Would you like to pick out one piece of candy?

FRANKIE: One piece of candy?

GROCER: Your change comes to just enough. I have thirty-one pieces left. Guess circus folk don't much like candy. Go ahead and choose one.

(*The Grocer holds a box of candy down for Frankie. After careful consideration, Frankie chooses one, which finds its way immediately into Frankie's pocket.*)

Well now, go ahead and hurry on home, before that butter melts. Have a nice day.

FRANKIE: Thank you!

(Frankie happily takes the bag and heads home, walking at a brisk, determined pace. Almost immediately Frankie encounters the Mail Carrier, squatting on the ground and hunting through the mailbag, tossing letters left and right.)

MAIL CARRIER: Howdy, Frankie! Thanks again for your help!

(Frankie waves and hurries by. Next, Frankie encounters the New Parent, still pushing the carriage back and forth.

NEW PARENT: Oh, hello, Frankie! Thanks again for your help! She's still asleep!

(Frankie waves and hurries by. Next, Frankie encounters the Shopkeeper, now arranging a display of barrels.)

SHOPKEEPER: Well, hello, young Frankie! Thanks again for your help. Let me know if you need any barrels!

(Frankie waves and hurries by. Next, Frankie encounters the children with their jump rope. This time Parker and Jody spin the rope as Cory jumps.)

CORY: Hi, Frankie!

PARKER: Thanks again, Frankie!

(Frankie waves and hurries home. Mom appears, perhaps with a counter or table.)

MOM: Oh, there you are, Frankie! I was starting to wonder whether you'd been eaten by bears. Did you get those groceries for me?

(Frankie proudly proffers the grocery bag, which Mom takes. Mom sets the bag down on the floor or the table and goes through it.)

Now let's see what you remembered to get, Frankie. A dozen eggs…

(She pulls them out, somewhat surprised.)

…a pound of butter…

(She pulls it out, with growing astonishment.)

…and two pints of milk!

(She pulls it out, amazed.)

Why, Frankie…

(Words fail her. Frankie takes out the piece of candy and unwraps it.)

FRANKIE: And one piece of candy!

(Frankie eats the candy. Mom hugs Frankie.)

(End of play.)

PS_BX08060074

CreateSpace
222 Old Wire Rd
Columbia, SC 29172

Question About Your Order?
Log in to your account at www.createspace.com and "Contact Support."

08/21/2018 12:15:12 PM
Order ID: 235561395

Qty.	Item

IN THIS SHIPMENT

1   It's Elementary!
         1620888009

The Author Speaks

What inspired you to write this play?
I'm not sure. It rattled around in my head for more than a year before I got it out. I suspect I caught myself reciting my grocery list in my head (maybe I moved my lips) and the idea just bloomed. I love the "whisper down the lane" way the list changes. It chimes with something I always told my casts when I was directing: Practice doesn't always make perfect. Practice makes permanent. Only perfect practice makes perfect.

Was the structure or other elements of the play influenced by any other work?
Definitely. I very consciously borrowed the repetitive language and structure found in folktales like *The Three Little Pigs* and *Goldilocks and the Three Bears.* For example, everyone says to Frankie, "If you're not in a hurry." The circular structure that ends where it began is also found all over literature.

Have you dealt with the same theme in other works that you have written?
Frankie might not be the brightest child, but Frankie wants to help. Frankie wants to be useful. Even the mistakes Frankie makes come as a result of trying to help other people out. I think there's something of the "trying my very best, not sure it's good enough" vibe in most of my protagonists.

What writers have had the most profound effect on your style?
Writing this play, I suppose I had Dr. Seuss and Mother Goose chiefly in mind. Most of my work owes more to the likes of Oscar Wilde and P.G. Wodehouse. I love writers who can hear the music in words. In one way, I guess *Frankie Gets It Right* is very Oscar Wilde, in that it's art for art's sake—it doesn't

really try to teach any lesson.

What do you hope to achieve with this work?
Ten minutes of silly fun. A rebuttal to "nice guys finish last." Frankie's eagerness to help is the whole problem—but it's *not* a problem because the universe comes to the rescue. Niceness is rewarded. But mostly ten minutes of silly fun.

What were the biggest challenges involved in the writing of this play?
All the challenges were self-imposed. I decided early in the writing process that Frankie would say *only* the grocery list (I later added "please" and "thank you") so I had to figure out how to make that work. I also—for no real reason—decided that all of the characters except Mom would be pronounless in the stage directions. I wanted nothing to even hint that I had any preference as to the gender of any character. That was hard work, as was thinking up all the genderless names. Also, I wanted a clear echo effect from one scene to the next, yet I wanted each person Frankie encountered to have a distinct voice. That was a tough balance to achieve.

What are the most common mistakes that occur in productions of your work?
Ad-libbing. Sure, if someone drops a line or the scenery falls down, ad-libbing can save the day and I'm all for it. But there's a reason I chose exactly the words I did. I'm a musician as well as a writer and I pay close attention to the shape and rhythm of language. I've been known to change "no, it's not" to "no, it isn't" in the middle of a production because I think the music is better. It's not enough to get the gist of the line—try to say the actual words the playwright wrote.

What inspired you to become a playwright?
The fact that young people are much better actors than most of us know. So many school theatre productions put demands on

young actors that no one would ever expect a professional actor to cope with—inadequate rehearsal time, characters absurdly removed from the actors' own experience, etc. And sure, they "pull it off" more times than not. But when young actors get the opportunity to perform work that is really right for them, their parents and their peers are stunned—and so are they. Who knew they could act that well? I write for young performers to spread that feeling all over the world.

How did you research the subject?
I didn't have to. I've been buying my own groceries for years now.

Are any characters modeled after real life or historical figures?
Everyone has known a baby who would only sleep in a moving stroller. Other than that, no.

What is your writing process?
NOTICE: Mixed metaphors ahead. Proceed at your own risk.

My brain is a jungle. I'll get an idea—a spark—"repeating the list out loud over and over so as not to forget it"—and it will just kind of bang around in my head, amongst a zillion other sparks, most of which will never be flames. Maybe as it bumps around it grows. "What if other numbers creep in and change the list?" Eventually it will get big enough or irritating enough that I have to pull it out and deal with it—or else it's been in there for a year attracting no attention and suddenly I have a project and I need it. It's the same with music. Anytime I'm near a keyboard (or really anything capable of making musical notes happen) I can't help "noodling." Little fragments of tunes are born, and bounce around in my head for months or years, until they either get too big to ignore or suddenly look useful. Then once I've pulled something out, I become obsessed and a first draft generally happens pretty fast. You do NOT want to try to talk to me during this process—trust me. Once that's done, I deliberately go and do something else for a while, and then come back to it with fresh eyes. Most of it generally turns out to be garbage, but I can usually dig out the core and make it work. Then it's just gradually tightening and trimming. Every paintbrush is smaller than the last.

Shakespeare gave advice to the players in *Hamlet*; if you could give advice to your cast what would it be?
Go big or go home. All of the characters in this play—even the adults—are enthusiastically grabbing for that brass ring. Hanging up that sign is the proudest moment in the shopkeeper's life! Finding number 31 is an unprecedented triumph for the mail carrier! The new parent's feet have never been sorer, and never felt such relief!

About the Author

Matt Buchanan is a New England-based professional playwright, composer and director specializing in theatre with and for young people. His more than two dozen published plays and musicals have been performed across the United States and on every continent but Antarctica. He has directed more than one hundred productions with young casts and is the author of *Directing Kids: A Comprehensive How-To Manual for Directors of Plays and Musicals with Casts of Young People from a Veteran Drama Teacher and Director*, published by YouthPLAYS. He is also an accomplished musician and multi-instrumentalist. Matt has a BA in Music from Harvard College and an MFA in Child Drama from the University of Texas at Austin. His website is www.childdrama.com.

SMART KID

by Meredith Dayna Levy

CAST OF CHARACTERS

JAMIE, elementary school age (9-11) and dyslexic. Any gender.

FRANKIE, Jamie's friend, also of elementary school age (9 -11). Any gender.

MR./MS. PATTERSON, Jamie's teacher. Any gender, any age.

NURSE BERKLEY, the school nurse. Any gender, any age.

MR./MS. DRIVER, Jamie's school bus driver. Any gender, any age.

RICK, Jamie's dad. Male, any age.

JOANNE, Jamie's mom. Female, any age.

PHOENIX, Jamie's neighbor, a year older than Jamie. Any gender.

Note: a diversity of races is encouraged. She/her pronouns are used as default, but most of these roles are gender neutral and can be played by males or nonbinary/trans persons, as well as females.

SETTING

The present. An unspecified American town or city.

DEDICATION

To Patricia Brooks Cope-Levy and the students at Oakland School in Keswick, VA.

(Lights up on a bare stage.)

(Standing downstage facing the audience is JAMIE, elementary school age [anywhere from 9-11].)

(Orbiting around Jamie are JOANNE, Jamie's mother; RICK, Jamie's father; MR./MS. PATTERSON, Jamie's teacher; NURSE BERKLEY, the school nurse; MR./MS. DRIVER, the bus driver; FRANKIE, Jamie's best friend; and PHOENIX, Jamie's neighbor. They all face upstage.)

(All characters should engage in dialogue facing the audience, never each other.)

JAMIE: *(Making a phone with her hand:)* Ring, ring, ring!

(She "hangs up.")

(Frankie turns to face downstage and addresses the audience.)

FRANKIE: Hey Jamie! Missed you on Friday. Where were you?

JAMIE: Home.

FRANKIE: You were sick or something?

JAMIE: Totally. Dad took me to the doctor and he said that I was "exhibiting the stress levels of a thirty-five year old."

FRANKIE: Whoa, that sounds serious.

JAMIE: Best part was that I wasn't allowed to do any of my homework.

FRANKIE: But our book reports are due today!

JAMIE: It's OK. I have a doctor's note.

(Frankie turns upstage, and Mr./Ms. Patterson turns downstage.)

MR./MS. PATTERSON: I know it's no fun to be sick, but you had a whole month to read this book. Just because you were sick the weekend before it was due doesn't excuse you from having to do it. I want your report on my desk by the end of the day tomorrow.

JAMIE: But Mr./Ms. Patterson —!

MR./MS. PATTERSON: No excuses, no exceptions. You're a smart kid, Jamie. I know you can do this.

> *(Mr./Ms. Patterson turns upstage, and Nurse Berkley turns downstage.)*

NURSE BERKLEY: Where does it hurt?

JAMIE: My tummy.

NURSE BERKLEY: Did you eat too much candy at lunch?

JAMIE: No.

> *(Nurse Berkley takes Jamie's temperature.)*

NURSE BERKLEY: You don't have a fever. This wouldn't happen to be because you didn't do your book report? Mr./Ms. Patterson told me that you got upset with her about it this morning.

JAMIE: Can you keep a secret?

NURSE BERKLEY: Nurse-patient confidentiality.

JAMIE: I did do my book report, but a kid on the bus stole it.

NURSE BERKLEY: Somebody *stole* your book report?

JAMIE: I didn't want to tell Mr./Ms. Patterson because it's embarrassing when *a bully* steals your stuff, and the bus driver totally ignores everything.

> *(Nurse Berkley turns upstage, and Mr./Ms. Driver turns downstage.)*

MR./MS. DRIVER: Are you accusing me of not running a tight ship here, kid?

JAMIE: What do you mean, a tight ship? This is a bus.

MR./MS. DRIVER: That Nurse Berkley told me some bully nicked your book report on *my* bus, and that I'd better keep an eye out.

JAMIE: Can you keep a secret? No one stole my book report. I didn't write it because I had important appointments to keep last weekend.

(Phoenix turns downstage; he is dressed in pirate garb.)

PHOENIX: C'mon, it's time to play pirates!

JAMIE: I can't, Phoenix. I've got this book report to write.

PHOENIX: That won't take long.

JAMIE: I haven't finished reading the book.

PHOENIX: Then it might take you a bit longer. *(Looks over her shoulder at the book:)* Oh, I read that book last summer.

JAMIE: Can you tell me about it? Then I wouldn't have to finish reading it.

PHOENIX: I don't remember all the details. I just remember it was pretty funny.

JAMIE: There's nothing funny about it. It's too hard to read, and I don't even know half these words!

PHOENIX: When is it due?

JAMIE: Tomorrow.

PHOENIX: So watch the movie on YouTube. That's what my brother Mark does—and everyone says he's a genius. Now c'mon, Frankie is gonna be home any minute. Do you really want to let those water balloons we made yesterday go to waste?

(Jamie contemplates, then closes the book.)

JAMIE: Ahoy, maties!

PHOENIX: *(Charging upstage:)* Shiver me timbers!

MR./MS. DRIVER: I see. Very important appointments.

JAMIE: Yes. And then I had to call my dad because he wants to talk to me every day when he's traveling. *(Makes phone with her hand:)* Ring, ring, ring!

   (Rick turns downstage.)

RICK: *(Making a phone with his hand, picking up:)* Hey there, Jam-ster. Everything okay?

JAMIE: I just need help with my book report.

RICK: I'm sorry, but I can't help you right now. I'm working. Maybe in a couple days, when I'm home again.

JAMIE: It's due tomorrow.

RICK: Why don't you ask your mother to help you?

   (Joanne turns downstage; she is folding laundry and watching TV.)

JOANNE: Honey, can't you see I'm busy?

JAMIE: You're just watching TV.

JOANNE: I'm also folding laundry.

JAMIE: I need help with this book report. Can't you read it to me?

JOANNE: You're getting a little old for me to keep reading out loud to you. *(To the TV:)* C'mon, Simon, cut the girl some slack. She's an orphan, for cripes' sake!

JAMIE: If Dad were here, he would read it to me!

JOANNE: Well, he isn't here, and frankly, I think he is coddling you too much. You're a smart kid, Jamie; you can read that book by yourself now.

JAMIE: Fine. If you won't read it to me, then will you take me to the library so I can get the audio book?

JOANNE: Absolutely not. You can read the actual book like everybody else.

JAMIE: Reading gives me a headache.

JOANNE: Well, I don't know what to tell you, kid. We all have to do things that give us headaches sometimes. Like laundry. Or parenting.

(Joanne turns upstage.)

JAMIE: *(Back on phone:)* She's too busy to help me either.

RICK: Chin up, Jam-ster. You're a smart kid; I know you can handle this. Read it out loud to yourself and pretend that I'm reading to you. Got to go! Love you!

(Rick turns upstage.)

MR./MS. DRIVER: I'm not saying that talking to your dad or playing pirates with your neighbor aren't important things. But a lot of people would say your school work is as important as that stuff. You're a smart kid—

JAMIE: WHY DOES EVERYONE KEEP SAYING THAT?!

(All characters look at Jamie; those facing upstage maybe turn over their shoulder to look.)

MR./MS. DRIVER: Sorry, kid.

(All characters turn back upstage, except for Frankie.)

FRANKIE: What's going on? You're lying to everyone! You told Nurse Berkley someone stole your book report, you told the bus driver that your mom wouldn't read to you—

JAMIE: She wouldn't—!

FRANKIE: You told me that you were too sick to do it.

JAMIE: I was.

FRANKIE: Those are three different stories, Jamie! What *actually* happened!?

JAMIE: Fine. You really want to know?

FRANKIE: Yes!

JAMIE: You really want to?

FRANKIE: Yes!

JAMIE: ...Aliens stole my book.

FRANKIE: Aliens.

JAMIE: They made me swear I wouldn't tell anyone.

FRANKIE: I'm your best friend. You don't think I notice things?

(All characters surround Jamie.)

MR./MS. DRIVER: Can you read that sign ahead of me?

NURSE BERKLEY: Jamie, I asked you to grab the Tums from the cabinet, not the Advil. Can't you read?

FRANKIE: Like how you seem to get a coughing fit every time you're asked to read out loud?

MR./MS. DRIVER: I hate detours. What does that street sign say, kid?

RICK: Keep working hard, okay Jam-ster? Make me proud.

FRANKIE: Or how lousy you are at word search games?

JOANNE: It's just a book, honey. It's not going to bite you.

PHOENIX: *(Running across the stage:)* Talley-ho! What does the map say? Which way do we need to go next?

FRANKIE: Or how you cheat on spelling tests?

NURSE BERKLEY: Can you see these letters, on the chart here?

JAMIE: *(Covering one eye:)* E?

NURSE BERKLEY: F.

JAMIE: N?

NURSE BERKLEY: M.

JAMIE: D?

NURSE BERKLEY: B. You might need to get some glasses, Jamie.

JAMIE: Glasses are for people who can't see. But I can see the baseball coming at me in the field, I can see the bird's nest outside my window, I can see the billboard pictures on the highway when I drive to school. I can see just fine!

(All the other characters turn upstage, except Mr./Ms. Patterson.)

MR./MS. PATTERSON: I appreciate you turning in your report. Better late then never. You made some excellent points and had some great ideas. But there's a problem. Well, two problems. The first is that it's based on the movie, not the book. I've seen the movie, and there are some big differences.

JAMIE: I couldn't read the whole book in time.

MR./MS. PATTERSON: Which leads me to the second problem. There are lots of words spelled wrong in this report.

JAMIE: I'm not a good speller. My dad usually helps me.

MR./MS. PATTERSON: Are you sure that's all it is? That you're a bad speller? Because I think it might be bigger than that.

JAMIE: Are you calling me stupid?

MR./MS. PATTERSON: Absolutely not.

JAMIE: Because I'm a smart kid—everyone says so.

MR./MS. PATTERSON: Your friend Frankie came and talked to me during recess today.

JAMIE: I don't know what s/he told you, but whatever it is, it isn't true!

MR./MS. PATTERSON: Can you tell me what's true, Jamie?

(As Jamie speaks, each character on stage, including Mr./Ms. Patterson, turns to face Jamie.)

JAMIE: Letters jump around on the page—doing somersaults and flips—every time I look at them. They move so fast I can't keep up. My head hurts, my tummy hurts, and you can say I'm making it up, but I'm not. I know my eyes work just fine. I see everything else the same as everyone else, but when I try to read, the letters run away from me and *that's the truth.*

(All characters now face Jamie. It is as if they are all seeing her anew.)

(Blackout. End of play.)

The Author Speaks

What inspired you to write this play?

I was inspired to write this play by my wife, Patricia Brooks Cope-Levy. She is dyslexic and struggled with reading as a child. She hid her learning disability for several years before she was diagnosed in the second grade. I felt it was important to put dyslexia onstage as a way of elevating awareness in the community, as well as validating the experiences of many young people who may feel isolated or lonely because of their disability.

Was the structure or other elements of the play influenced by any other work?

Jamie's wild imagination and artful storytelling was sparked by my love of the *Calvin and Hobbes* comics, written by Bill Watterson. The concept of a perceived reality vs. the actual reality is one of my many points of fascination with the comic strip series, and I felt inspired to write a character who is straddling a similar divide with something more internal, like a disability. While dyslexia is not nearly as much fun as a stuffed tiger, Jamie is working to justify her coping mechanisms and maintain her own sense of security and reality.

The convention of the characters addressing the audience primarily was also a deliberate choice. Firstly, the direct address is a quick way to immerse the audience and involve them in the drama of the play; when you only have ten minutes, you need to make every minute count! Moreover, Jamie is not truly seen by her community until she voices the truth about her condition. Frankie and the teacher come the closest, as they have suspicions about why Jamie hasn't written her book report, but even they see Jamie anew upon her confession at the end of the play.

Have you dealt with the same theme in other works that you have written?

Where this work resonates most with other plays I have written is in the struggle to acknowledge and embrace one's whole and true self—even the parts of ourselves we don't like so much. In **Smart Kid**, Jamie doesn't understand why her eyes read letters differently, but she knows that they do, and she has not embraced that difference. Only at the end, when she is truly seen, when she has given voice to her own truth, will she be able to do so. In this play, we don't necessarily see Jamie come to a place of self-love, but the potential is palpable at the end. And that potential for self-love and a return to authenticity is present in all of my work: **She Made Space** is a one-woman show about a young woman's embracing of her sexuality; **Decision Height** is an ensemble show where we witness the process of self-actualization occur in multiple characters. **Coupler** is a comedy that focuses on a man who is learning to grow up and embrace reality over his fantasies of what life should be.

What writers have had the most profound effect on your style?

I think it's impossible to engage with a play and not be affected in some way by their style; but certainly the works of Tennessee Williams, Beth Henley and Caryl Churchill. All three of these playwrights serve poetic truth over physical truth. Many of their plays can seem outlandish or "unrealistic," even as they are performed in a "realistic" way, with set pieces and period clothes and contemporary dialogue. But they are not seeking to recreate a historical truth, or portray a physical one; instead they strive to evoke an emotional truth that impacts the audience. I try with all my plays to do the same—it doesn't matter to me if the physicality of the space or the characters are realistic (i.e. people address the audience directly in *Smart Kid*), so long as the emotional truth conveyed is genuine.

What do you hope to achieve with this work?
I hope to provide a space for young people to engage with theatre, and explore what it means to have a learning disability and the social stigmas and isolation that can arise when empathy and understanding are lacking. Not everyone is dyslexic, but everyone has *something* about themselves they don't like, or that they feel makes them weak, or different. The emotional truth of Jamie's experience is what I hope both the audience and those creating the play walk away with. Theatre is a wonderful vehicle for modeling empathy, and it is my hope that this play can be one of many experiences that impress upon young people the importance of authenticity and embracing one's *whole* self.

What were the biggest challenges involved in the writing of this play?
On one level, I would say the biggest challenge was honoring my wife's experience while recognizing that dyslexia affects lots of people differently, and to varying degrees. The physical truths of one's experience don't always translate, or even seem realistic, to someone else. But the emotional truth of one's experience is often more universal and accessible to those whose life experience is different than your own. Finding that balance is always tricky, and was definitely a challenge with this play.

However, I would also share that, as this is my first play for young actors and young audiences, I also experienced challenges in writing dialogue that was both comfortable and compelling in the mouths and ears of children. Oftentimes I was elevating the language in a way that was not authentic to the experience of young adolescence. Working with children on both the first commissioned production and the second classroom exercise was pretty important to the writing process, as was my recent service as a Sunday school teacher. Hearing children talk and engage with the story each Sunday has been really eye opening to me not only in terms of how children talk, but how they communicate big feelings and ideas through the stories they construct.

What are the most common mistakes that occur in productions of your work?
I think the most common mistake that people make when producing my work is that they do not emphasize the importance of learning the lines as they are written. Often paraphrasing happens, or lines get dropped over the course of the rehearsal and are never identified and put back in. The dialogue is the most important tool the playwright provides to the production team; it can help to create the world of the play and these characters, in the same way that a set or costumes do.

Similarly, the punctuation of the dialogue (dashes, commas, etc.) also telegraphs a lot about how I as the playwright recommend the actor and director approach the dialogue. If the actor wants to yell a certain line, but there is no "!" present, then I would hope the director and the actor have a conversation about what that impulse is that the actor is feeling and where (or where not) it is justified in the text of the play. I think sometimes punctuation gets ignored, or is not seen as important.

What inspired you to become a playwright?
As a kid, I never thought very much about the people who wrote the plays. My first reckoning of that reality came in high school when I had to write a one-act play for a scriptwriting class, and I suddenly became aware of the awesome power and responsibility that comes with crafting a story meant to be embodied and performed. It felt like playing God, in a way,

and I loved the idea of crafting the play without actually being *in* the play. In college, playwriting transitioned from "a fun thing I did sometimes" to being my primary vocation within the theatre, because I discerned that playwriting was the medium through which I could most authentically communicate and engage with the world.

As a person of faith, it's also important to me that I write plays that compel audiences to consider how they are treating one another, and how they choose to move through the world. I believe there are many paths to God—and while the physical practices of differing faiths may look different, I believe the emotional truths that those teachings seek to instruct us on are often the same. I write with the intention to offer yet another path to those ideals.

Are any characters modeled after real life or historical figures?
Jamie is very loosely based on my wife, Patricia Brooks Cope-Levy. She was a studious student and never would have skipped a book report to play pirates! The teacher is based on my fourth-grade teacher, Dr. Pepe. She was very serious, and she intimidated me as a child; I also wrote my first book report for her class! I had great and really present and supportive parents—so Jamie's parents are based on what my nightmare parents would have been as a child. Everyone else is a compilation of people I knew and archetype roles I've identified as being present in my life.

Shakespeare gave advice to the players in *Hamlet*; if you could give advice to your cast what would it be?
1.) A play should never be such a serious thing that you don't derive any joy from the experience. It's not enough to just put on the play. The quality of the rehearsal period inevitably trickles down into the final product, and I think it's important to emphasize throughout the process that we are creating an

event that can be shared with others.

2.) It can be scary to speak in front of a lot of people, and pretend to be someone else. But by sharing stories on stage, you are helping to teach other people how to be empathetic and think about the experiences of others. The risks you are taking on stage may help someone take a risk in their own life, and that's such a great gift to give!

3.) Learn all of the lines as best you can as they've been written. Sometimes it's easier to paraphrase, but the playwright often writes a line a certain way to get a specific message or feeling across. They are working to make distinct voices, and often the vocabulary of a character, or their diction and syntax patterns, can tell you a lot about who that character is. So do your best to learn the lines as they've been written.

How was the first production different from the vision that you created in your mind?
I wrote the first draft of this play specifically for a group of actors who would perform it as part of a benefit concert my wife and I produced called "Legend," which featured several dances and short plays. My vision for the play was strongly dictated by the realities of the commission. Many of our actors had never worked with a new play, or *been* in a play for that matter. Our space for the performance was a church, with no hidden exits and a narrow "stage" space at the front. Hence, we kept everyone on stage the whole play, direct address helped minimize movement or blocking, and we had next to no props and simple costumes.

My vision has evolved in nuance since that first production. Now I see specific costuming and props, a wide expanse that the actors take up with their bodies, moving in space — especially a swirl of bodies surrounding Jamie during the colliding of challenges with reading toward the end of the play. I see lighting that helps us to focus on which actor is speaking and that expands as the play progresses as more and more of the truth comes to light.

Should Jamie be played by a boy or a girl?
I think, in today's world, anytime we can elevate those groups of people who are often underrepresented, we should. I think it is fine for Jamie to be played by a boy. But I think there are lots of plays about boys already. If Jamie could be played by a girl, or by someone who is questioning their gender, or is transgender, or who maybe identifies as gender-queer…then I think that's awesome!

About the Author

Meredith Dayna Levy writes plays to give a platform to quiet, quirky and queer voices, as well as make space for dynamic, challenging women on stage. Her plays *Decision Height*, *Coupler* and *She Made Space* have all received awards and commendations from the Kennedy Center American College Theatre Festival. Her ten-minute play *Waiting for Sylvia* has been produced in festivals at colleges around the country. *Smart Kid* is her first play for young audiences. She received her B.A. in theatre from Hollins University, and her M.F.A. in Playwriting from the Hollins Playwright's Lab in 2018. She is a proud member of the Dramatists Guild.

CAKE FOR THE QUEEN
by Robin Blasberg

CAST OF CHARACTERS

KING, the head of the castle; relies on others for ideas and decisions; adores the Queen.

QUEEN, co-head of the castle; has no patience and is only interested in appearances.

COUNSEL, the King's royal advisor; very confident.

MAID, the brains of the castle; employed as a servant.

TOWN CRIER, announcer of all of the King's proclamations.

SHIRLEY SUGARHOUSE, first cake contestant.

BETTY BAKER, second cake contestant.

ROSEMARY HONEYGRAHAM, third cake contestant.

ROBIN HOODWINKLE, outlaw masquerading as a cake contestant.

THE CROWD, people from the town and surrounding villages.

NOTE

Dialogue marked as THE CROWD may be assigned to one or more individuals as fits the needs of your production.

(As the lights come up, the TOWN CRIER stands at attention just outside the doorway of the King's chamber, inside of which is the QUEEN. The MAID is also inside the chamber, dusting the King's throne. The CROWD can be seen going about their daily business in the town square. The town square includes tables with fruit and wares where the Crowd is buying and selling goods.)

QUEEN: *(To Maid:)* And be sure to shine the mirror so that I can marvel at my reflection when I return. I will be back after my meeting with the Gossip Exchange. Oh, I do hope that witless man comes up with a good idea for my birthday while I'm gone.

MAID: Witless man?

QUEEN: The King!!! Whom else would I be referring to?

(Queen exits, shaking her head.)

MAID: It's a pity the King only listens to blustery blokes who wear fine clothes and strut around, and I am merely a lowly maid.

(Maid begins to shine mirror.)

But I am so grateful for this job. I do what I can to keep in good standing with everyone.

(Maid sighs and speaks dreamily.)

Alas, if only I could be queen for a day.

(The KING enters the room with COUNSEL. The King begins walking back and forth.)

KING: Tomorrow is the Queen's birthday. She deserves a scrumptious cake in her honor. *(Rubbing his belly:)* Counsel, how can I ensure that the Queen has the most delectable cake in all the land?

COUNSEL: Ahem. Let me confer for a moment.

(Counsel turns his back to the King. He moves his mouth as if talking to himself. He looks at the palm of one hand and then the other.)

KING: Counsel? What say ye?

(Counsel raises his hand to signal quiet.)

COUNSEL: I am in heavy thought.

(He shuts his eyes and begins to hum softly. While dusting Counsel's feet, Maid whispers to Counsel.)

MAID: Cake contest.

(Counsel raises one finger in the air and turns around to face the King.)

COUNSEL: I've got it!

KING: Yes, good Counsel?

COUNSEL: A cake contest!

KING: What a splendid idea!

COUNSEL: Yes. I know.

KING: Good man.

COUNSEL: I'm brilliant.

MAID: Oh, I'm feeling a wave of hot air. I need to step outside to catch my breath.

(Maid fans herself as she exits.)

KING: Have the Town Crier inform the masses.

COUNSEL: *(Turning to Town Crier:)* Town Crier, inform the masses.

(Town Crier runs to town square.)

TOWN CRIER: Hear ye! Hear ye! In honor of the Queen's impending birthday, the Kingdom of Confection will be hosting a royal cake competition. All worthy bakers near and far, young and old, must prepare their most delectable cakes for the contest tomorrow.

> *(Crowd looks at each other, nods, then shouts together.)*

THE CROWD: Why should we? What's in it for us?

TOWN CRIER: *(Shrugs.)* I will have to inquire.

> *(Crowd goes back to what they were doing beforehand. Town Crier enters the King's chamber.)*

It appears that the masses will require an incentive to encourage their participation.

KING: Counsel? What say ye?

COUNSEL: Ahem. One moment.

> *(Counsel turns his back to the King and scans the room for Maid, who is not there. Counsel taps finger to cheek.)*

KING: Quickly, Counsel! The masses are waiting.

> *(Counsel raises one finger in the air and turns around to face the King.)*

COUNSEL: I've got it!

KING: Yes, good Counsel?

COUNSEL: The winner will receive the illustrious title of "Pastry Chef Supreme."

KING: What a splendid idea!

COUNSEL: Yes. I've done it again.

KING: Good man.

COUNSEL: This is why I am your prized advisor.

KING: Yes, 'tis true. *(Pause.)* Counsel, have the Town Crier inform the masses.

COUNSEL: Town Crier, inform the masses.

(Town Crier races to the town square and speaks again to Crowd.)

TOWN CRIER: Hear ye! Hear ye! By declaration of the King, the winner of the cake contest will receive the illustrious title of "Pastry Chef Supreme."

(Crowd looks at each other, nods, then shouts together.)

THE CROWD: That's it? Forget it.

(Crowd goes back to what they were doing. Maid reenters chamber carrying a pail and scrub brush. She begins to scrub the floor.)

TOWN CRIER: *(Stepping back into the King's chamber:)* It appears that an illustrious title will not motivate the masses.

KING: Counsel, what could they want?

(Counsel turns his back to the King and taps finger to cheek. While scrubbing the floor in front of Counsel, Maid whispers to Counsel.)

MAID: Twenty gold coins.

(Counsel raises one finger in the air and turns around to face the King.)

COUNSEL: I've got it!

KING: Yes, good Counsel?

COUNSEL: Twenty gold coins.

KING: What a splendid idea!

COUNSEL: Yes. I amaze myself sometimes.

MAID: *(Coughing loudly:)* Excuse me. There must have been a foul wind passing by.

KING: Counsel, have the Town Crier inform the masses.

COUNSEL: Town Crier, inform the masses.

(Town Crier races to the town square and speaks again to Crowd.)

TOWN CRIER: Hear ye! Hear ye! The King will offer twenty gold coins to the winner of the cake contest.

THE CROWD: Hooray! Money talks. We'll do it.

(Crowd pairs up and runs offstage shouting.)

Come on! Fire up the ovens. We need to get baking.

(Lights dim.)

(Lights rise and the King can be seen outside.)

KING: What a glorious morning! I can taste the sweetness of the day already.

(Queen is in the chamber as King enters.)

QUEEN: How do I look?

KING: Lovely, as always.

QUEEN: That's precisely what I want to hear.

(Queen turns to the mirror to primp herself as King speaks.)

KING: My dear Queen, you will be so pleased. We are having a cake contest in your honor. The best bakers in the kingdom will be bringing you their most delectable cakes.

(He rubs his belly.)

QUEEN: What a wonderful idea!

KING: I know. *(He bats his eyelashes.)* Only the best for you.

QUEEN: Wait till the other kingdoms hear about this! *(Seriously:)* So, where are they?

KING: Where are what?

QUEEN: The cakes. Where are they?

KING: Oh, well…

QUEEN: Come now.

(She claps her hands twice.)

You know the saying, "Early to rise, eat the best pies."

KING: Huh?

QUEEN: It means, "Let's get this show on the road."

(She claps her hands twice again.)

KING: *(Hustling to the door:)* Counsel, have the Town Crier summon the cakes.

COUNSEL: *(Appearing at the door and turning to the Town Crier beside him:)* Town Crier, summon the cakes.

(Town Crier races to the town square.)

TOWN CRIER: Hear ye! Hear ye! May all participants in the royal bakery contest present their cakes.

THE CROWD: Here come the best bakers in the kingdom.

(SHIRLEY SUGARHOUSE, BETTY BAKER and ROSEMARY HONEYGRAHAM march forward with their cakes. The Crowd lines the procession.)

Look! There's Shirley Sugarhouse.

SHIRLEY SUGARHOUSE: My name is Shirley Sugarhouse, and this is my Utterly Awesome Almond Angel Food Cake.

(She places her cake on the table in the town square.)

THE CROWD: Ooooh.

THE CROWD: They'll go nuts over that heavenly delight.

THE CROWD: Look! There's Betty Baker.

BETTY BAKER: My name is Betty Baker, and this is my Betty Baker Butter Bomb cake.

(She places her cake on the table in the town square.)

THE CROWD: Aaaah.

THE CROWD: That'll really churn up the votes.

THE CROWD: Look! There's Rosemary Honeygraham.

ROSEMARY HONEYGRAHAM: My name is Rosemary Honeygraham, and this is my Seismic Savory Cinnamon Shortcake.

(She places her cake on the table in the town square.)

THE CROWD: Ooooh.

THE CROWD: That'll shake up the competition for sure.

THE CROWD: Yup. *(To the audience, shaking their heads:)* It wasn't even worth cracking an egg knowing Shirley Sugarhouse, Betty Baker and Rosemary Honeygraham were competing.

TOWN CRIER: If that's all the contestants, then the judging will begin.

QUEEN: *(To King and Counsel:)* I'll stay here. I want to be surprised. Remember, only the most beautiful will be worthy of my honor. And don't take too long.

(Queen flips hourglass over on the table as King and Counsel go to the town square to inspect the cakes.)

ROBIN HOODWINKLE: *(Off:)* Wait!

THE CROWD: *(Looking around:)* Who's that?

(ROBIN HOODWINKLE runs onto the stage carrying a five-tiered cake.)

THE CROWD: Wow! That cake looks incredible!

ROBIN HOODWINKLE: Let me introduce myself. My name is Robin Hoodwinkle, and this is my Colossal King-Sized

Cream-o-lotta Crook Cake. This unbeatable cake has swept up riches from cake contests all over the world.

THE CROWD: Ooooo…

ROBIN HOODWINKLE: This cake is not just incredible! It's spectacular! It's phenomenal! It's…your winner.

THE CROWD: Ahhh…

(Maid is outside the doorway sweeping. She mutters to herself:)

MAID: Looks aren't everything. Gotta taste it to believe it.

QUEEN: *(Calling from inside the chamber:)* Maid! Maid! Come set the table.

(Maid goes inside and begins to set the table as Queen taps her fingers impatiently.)

TOWN CRIER: *(Turning to King and Counsel:)* Judges!

KING: *(To Counsel:)* Counsel, what say ye?

COUNSEL: Well! I think the winner here is obvious. The Colossal King-sized Cream-o-lotta Crook Cake has won cake contests all over the world. It's incredible! It's spectacular! It's phenomenal! It's…our winner.

KING: You're absolutely right.

COUNSEL: No doubt.

KING: Counsel, have the Town Crier inform the masses.

COUNSEL: Town Crier, inform the masses.

TOWN CRIER: *(To the Crowd:)* Hear ye! Hear ye! The winner of the King's Royal Cake Competition is… May we have a drumroll, please?

(Drumroll.)

The winner of the King's Royal Cake Competition is the Colossal King-sized Cream-o-lotta Crook Cake!

(Wild applause and cheers from the Crowd.)

KING: Counsel, I am returning to my chamber. Have the Town Crier bring forth the winning cake.

COUNSEL: Town Crier, bring forth the winning cake.

(Counsel follows King back to chamber.)

TOWN CRIER: *(To the Crowd:)* Hear ye! Hear ye! Bring forth the Colossal King-sized Cream-o-lotta Crook Cake!

ROBIN HOODWINKLE: *(Shouting:)* I will bring you the Colossal King-sized Cream-o-lotta Crook Cake. But first *you* must bring forth the twenty gold coins.

TOWN CRIER: *(Stepping back into the King's chamber:)* It seems the winner insists that he be brought the twenty gold coins *first* before he will hand over his cake.

KING: *(Irritated:)* Counsel, take care of this negotiation! Quick! The Queen is waiting.

(Counsel grabs a bag of gold coins from beside the King's chair and hurries to the town square. Robin Hoodwinkle stands in front of the table, blocking Counsel from reaching the cake.)

ROBIN HOODWINKLE: First, the gold.

COUNSEL: Yes. Yes, of course. *(Handing over the bag of gold coins:)* Congratulations!

ROBIN HOODWINKLE: *(Begins to count the coins in the bag.)* One, two, three, four, five…

COUNSEL: *(Clearing his throat:)* Ahem! The cake, please!

(Robin Hoodwinkle holds up one finger to demand silence.)

ROBIN HOODWINKLE: You should always check to make sure you haven't been short-changed.

COUNSEL: *(Crossing his arms and tapping his feet impatiently:)* You are testing my patience.

ROBIN HOODWINKLE: Sixteen, seventeen, eighteen, nineteen, twenty. It's all there. Thank you very much.

> *(Robin Hoodwinkle bows quickly to Counsel and then hurries off the stage with the bag of gold coins. Counsel grabs the cake and carries it into the King's chamber, setting it down on the table in front of the Queen.)*

KING: I now present you with…the winning cake.

THE CROWD: *(To Town Crier, who stands again in the town square:)* What about these other cakes?

TOWN CRIER: *(Shrugs.)* I will have to inquire.

> *(Town Crier enters the King's chamber.)*

The masses would like to know what to do with the other cakes.

KING: My dear Queen, what should we do with the other cakes?

QUEEN: The palace has no need for the losers. Give the remaining cakes to the masses. Let them eat cake!

KING: Counsel, have the Town Crier inform the masses.

COUNSEL: Town Crier, inform the masses.

TOWN CRIER: *(From town square:)* Hear ye! Hear ye! With regard to the remaining cakes, the Queen says, and I quote… *(Pauses dramatically.)* "LET THEM EAT CAKE!!!"

THE CROWD: Hooray!

> *(Crowd begins slicing the cakes and handing out pieces on plates. Meanwhile…)*

KING: Ah! The wonderful sound of the masses celebrating my dear Queen's birthday. It must be music to your ears, my Queen.

QUEEN: *(Ignoring the King's remark:)* Well, let's get on with it.

> *(The Queen claps her hands twice. The Maid lays a napkin across the Queen's lap.)*

Cut me a slice of this beauty.

> *(The Queen waits at the ready with fork in hand. The Maid cuts the cake. The cake immediately collapses. The Queen gasps.)*

My goodness! What has happened?

MAID: The cake fell apart.

QUEEN: The pieces look so stiff.

MAID: The cake is made of cardboard.

QUEEN: Cardboard? Whoever heard of that?

> *(Queen glares at King.)*

Didn't anyone *taste* this cake before it was declared the winner?

> *(King glares at Counsel.)*

KING: Counsel, why didn't you taste this cake before it was declared the winner?

COUNSEL: *(Embarrassed:)* Well, uh... That Robin Hoodwinkle!

KING: *(Begins to cry.)* It's the Queen's birthday, and she needs cake.

QUEEN: *(Looking at King:)* Save me from this embarrassment. Where are we going to get cake?

MAID: *(Handing the King a tissue:)* Outside. The masses are eating cake.

COUNSEL: To the town square for cake!

(The King and Queen follow Counsel to the town square.)

Coming through! Make way for royalty!

(Counsel, King and Queen push their way through to the cake table.)

THE CROWD: *(Standing in front of cake table:)* Sorry. You're too late. I just gave the last piece of cake away.

KING: *(Whining:)* But I've been looking so forward to eating cake.

QUEEN: What will the other kingdoms say? I'll be a laughingstock.

KING: Counsel, this is serious. We need cake.

SHIRLEY SUGARHOUSE: Did I hear you say you needed cake? Well, I am Shirley Sugarhouse. Not only do I make some of the finest cakes in town, but I also run a pastry school. And wouldn't you know it? I have a class starting in one hour. The cost is 40 gold coins. Every student will have completed one cake by the end of the afternoon.

KING: Counsel, you must attend the class.

COUNSEL: I…I…I am unprepared.

SHIRLEY SUGARHOUSE: Not to worry. No preparation is necessary. All supplies are included in the fee.

KING: *(Sternly:)* Counsel, this is an order. Go forth and make great cakes!

COUNSEL: As you wish.

(Counsel bows and exits with Shirley Sugarhouse.)

QUEEN: *(To King:)* This better end well.

(Queen crosses her arms. Meanwhile…Maid sits down at the King's table and looks out at the audience. Robin Hoodwinkle stands at the doorway peering inside. He holds a piece of cake.)

MAID: To have your cake and eat it too,
You can't just take what's said as true.
You need to taste it through and through.

(Robin Hoodwinkle steps into the room.)

ROBIN HOODWINKLE: What a lovely saying. I suppose you'd like to try a piece of cake then?

(He hands her a piece.)

My name is Robin Hoodwinkle. And, lovely lady, what may I call you?

MAID: The Maid.

ROBIN HOODWINKLE: Surely you are more than just the maid. A wise woman such as yourself must have a name.

MAID: Marian. My name is Maid Marian.

ROBIN HOODWINKLE: Well, Maid Marian, I've brought you a gold coin. I'm in the business of taking from the rich and giving to the poor.

MAID: Aren't you afraid of getting caught?

ROBIN HOODWINKLE: You're so practical. If only we all had your common sense. I aim to become a legendary outlaw, you see.

MAID: Robin Hoodwinkle, if you're striving for fame, I think you should shorten your name. Robin Hood, perhaps. It would have more of a ring to it.

ROBIN HOODWINKLE: Yes. Maid Marian, you've got quite a mind hiding beneath your rags. You are the Queen of Good Ideas. Well, I shouldn't stay long. Enjoy the cake, my Queen. I must run and hide in Sherwood Forest. Till we meet again, my clever lady.

(He tips his hat and exits. Maid sits down on the Queen's throne and takes a bite of cake.)

MAID: Hmm…me, the Queen of Good Ideas.

(She puffs out her chest with pride.)

It has a nice ring to it.

(Maid looks out at audience.)

Don't you think?

(End of play.)

The Author Speaks

What inspired you to write this play?

I've had many experiences in real life where people have been judged by their appearances, personality or rank. Many times, the most beautiful are judged by their exterior appearance, the most confident personalities are perceived to have the best ideas, and the lowest ranking person is undervalued. I wanted to create a play where these issues are brought to the forefront. I also wanted to do it in a lighthearted way rather than in a pedantic fashion.

Was the structure or other elements of the play influenced by any other work?

The silliness in this play was influenced by many Disney animated films which, even while dealing with serious subjects, never fail to include playful and humorous elements. Additionally, when I was in elementary school, we performed *Peter Pan*. I was impressed by how the production allowed for entire classes to have roles up on stage. I wanted to create a similar opportunity for other students who aren't cast as main characters to perform.

Have you dealt with the same theme in other works that you have written?

Yes. I wrote a middle school play, *The Music of Love*, that deals with a student being judged by his appearance. While thematically somewhat similar to *Cake for the Queen*, *The Music of Love* is a more intimate piece that depicts middle school students and not royalty. Also, while both *The Music of Love* and *Cake for the Queen* are comedies, the humor in *The Music of Love* is more whimsical in nature than that in *Cake for the Queen*. I felt that the style of humor in *Cake for the Queen* would be more appealing to a younger audience.

What writers have had the most profound effect on your style?

I would say that the playwright Neil Simon has influenced my work. In particular, Neil Simon's farce, **Rumors**, comes to mind. The over-the-top comedy in **Rumors** is also present in **Cake for the Queen**. Also, the ending of **Rumors** comes as a surprise, which I think is also the case in **Cake for the Queen**.

What do you hope to achieve with this work?

First of all, I hope that the performers and the audience have fun. I want people to laugh and enjoy the humor foremost. If the play's lesson of not judging by appearances is also absorbed, then that's an added bonus. I want people to try to remember that it's what's inside that counts.

What were the biggest challenges involved in the writing of this play?

The biggest challenge I had with this play was figuring out a suitable ending. Determining the Maid's role at the end of the play was particularly difficult. Additionally, some readers remarked that they wanted the Queen to be taught a lesson, but they still wanted her to get cake. They wanted both the royals and the townsfolk to live happily ever after. Other readers didn't want to see such a pat ending.

What inspired you to become a playwright?

I had been writing stories and poems for children's magazines when I happened to see a flyer for Try It Out Theatre at my local library. The theatre was looking for playwrights who would be interested in writing short scripts for their local readings. I decided to give it a try. When my first script was read to a packed audience, I was fascinated to see how the crowd reacted to my play. If it was supposed to be a funny line and no one laughed, I knew immediately that the line didn't work. With children's magazines, you are not present when your work is read, so you never have this opportunity to see how people respond to your work. Playwriting became a lot more appealing to me after that experience.

Are any characters modeled after real life or historical figures?
Some of the characters were influenced by real life or historical figures. The quote, "Let them eat cake" is the translation of a phrase often attributed to Marie Antoinette, the last Queen of France. These words were purportedly spoken by Marie Antoinette upon learning that the peasants were starving. Her callous response and the self-centered attitude that it reflects were used to develop the character of the Queen in *Cake for the Queen*. Additionally, the characters of Robin Hoodwinkle and Maid Marian refer to the legendary outlaw, Robin Hood, and his love, Maid Marian, respectively. Although Marie Antoinette, Robin Hood and Maid Marian are all historical figures, I did create my own spin on these characters for this play.

What is your writing process?
I always know the premise of a play before I sit down and write the first words. I may not have all of the characters and other details fleshed out, and I may not even know how the play ends, but I do know what the play will be about. In the case of *Cake for the Queen*, I knew that I wanted to write a play about a cake contest where the judges were going to determine the winner based solely on appearances. I also knew that I wanted the prettiest cake to taste the worst. The creation of the characters evolved as I went along. I find writing the first draft of any script to be the most difficult. Once I have a first draft down, though, I have a solid framework that I can refine and mold.

Shakespeare gave advice to the players in *Hamlet*; if you could give advice to your cast what would it be?
The line of communication between the King, Counsel and

Town Crier should be handled in a snappy manner. I realize that it is like using a messenger when a messenger isn't necessary. However, in addition to its comedic effect, the chain of communication also reveals the importance of rank and status of people in the royal household. The King would never deign to speak directly to the Town Crier. Similarly, the Town Crier knows that he can never speak to the King directly.

About the Author

Robin Blasberg writes plays, poems and short stories for all ages. Her play, ***The Music of Love***, was performed by students at Peekskill Middle School in Peekskill, New York. Her plays for older audiences have been presented at readings by Try It Out Theatre in Columbia, Maryland. Her poems and stories for young people have been published by *Highlights* and other children's magazines.

About YouthPLAYS

YouthPLAYS (www.youthplays.com) is a publisher of award-winning professional dramatists and talented new discoveries, each with an original theatrical voice, and all dedicated to expanding the vocabulary of theatre for young actors and audiences. On our website you'll find one-act and full-length plays and musicals for teen and pre-teen (and even college) actors, as well as duets and monologues for competition. Many of our authors' works have been widely produced at high schools and middle schools, youth theatres and other TYA companies, both amateur and professional, as well as at elementary schools, camps, churches and other institutions serving young audiences and/or actors worldwide. Most are intended for performance by young people, while some are intended for adult actors performing for young audiences.

YouthPLAYS was co-founded by professional playwrights Jonathan Dorf and Ed Shockley. It began merely as an additional outlet to market their own works, which included a substantial body of award-winning published and unpublished plays and musicals. Those interested in their published plays were directed to the respective publishers' websites, and unpublished plays were made available in electronic form. But when they saw the desperate need for material for young actors and audiences—coupled with their experience that numerous quality plays for young people weren't finding a home—they made the decision to represent the work of other playwrights as well. Dozens and dozens of authors are now members of the YouthPLAYS family, with scripts available both electronically and in traditional acting editions. We continue to grow as we look for exciting and challenging plays and musicals for young actors and audiences.

About ProduceaPlay.com

Let's put up a play! Great idea! But producing a play takes time, energy and knowledge. While finding the necessary time and energy is up to you, ProduceaPlay.com is a website designed to assist you with that third element: knowledge.

Created by YouthPLAYS' co-founders, Jonathan Dorf and Ed Shockley, ProduceaPlay.com serves as a resource for producers at all levels as it addresses the many facets of production. As Dorf and Shockley speak from their years of experience (as playwrights, producers, directors and more), they are joined by a group of award-winning theatre professionals and experienced teachers from the world of academic theatre, all making their expertise available for free in the hope of helping this and future generations of producers, whether it's at the school or university level, or in community or professional theatres.

The site is organized into a series of major topics, each of which has its own page that delves into the subject in detail, offering suggestions and links for further information. For example, Publicity covers everything from Publicizing Auditions to How to Use Social Media to Posters to whether it's worth hiring a publicist. Casting details Where to Find the Actors, How to Evaluate a Resume, Callbacks and even Dealing with Problem Actors. You'll find guidance on your Production Timeline, The Theater Space, Picking a Play, Budget, Contracts, Rehearsing the Play, The Program, House Management, Backstage, and many other important subjects.

The site is constantly under construction, so visit often for the latest insights on play producing, and let it help make your play production dreams a reality.

More from YouthPLAYS

K.C.@Bat by Zachary Israel Nobile Kampler (music) & Rocco Natale (book and lyrics)
Musical. 45-60 minutes. 4-7+ females, 1-5+ males (11-50+ performers possible).

Ernest Thayer's beloved poem about fictional baseball legend Casey and the town of Mudville springs to life in the present. Young K.C. moves from New York City to Mudville with her father and struggles to fit in...until, avid player that she is, she joins the down-and-out local baseball team and leads them all the way to the championship game, where she learns that there are things even more important than winning...

Of Plastic Things and Butterfly Wings by Greg Romero
Young Audiences. 45-50 minutes. 2-10 males, 3-10 females (2-20 performers possible).

A plastic water bottle named Sam has lost her parents in The Gyres, a swirling ocean landfill twice the size of Texas. With help from a blue crab with a giant claw, a parrot who thinks she is a seagull, and The Oldest Sea Turtle That Ever Lived, Sam embarks on a epic journey to save us all from the lonely, swirling vortex of thrown-away things and lost hope.

Calamity by E. J. C. Calvert
Comedy. 50-60 minutes. 3 females, 4-12+ either (7-15+ performers possible).

Twelve-year-old Calamity Jane and her mother are on their way to California when they find themselves in beleaguered Hoopersville. With all but a trio of townsfolk kidnapped by the hilariously hair-raising hoopsnakes, can Jane rally the remaining townspeople out of their hidey-holes to face the Hoopsnake Queen and rescue the populace, or will they too end up as dinner-in-waiting?

Kid Turboni Brings the Rain by Mark J. Costello
Dramedy. 60-70 minutes. 2 females, 3 males.

It's 115 degrees in the shade in Kid Turboni's Albuquerque housing project, and there's no end in sight. Tired of the heat's foolishness, Kid and his best friend Billy set out to liberate their people by stealing rain from Mother Nature just like their hero, fabled ex-tenant Smack Turkenson. Kid has bigger problems than the heat, though. He misses his mom, his friend Kelly wants to be more than friends, he can't get his rain dance right, and everyone's expectations for him are mighty hard to manage. It all crashes together as the temperature climbs, making everyone ask—can Kid Turboni bring the rain? Winner of the AATE Distinguished Play Award.

Scareville by Julia Edwards
Comedy with music for young audiences. 40-50 minutes. 3+ females, 2+ males (5+ gender-flexible performers possible).

Milo and Clare are afraid…of lots of things. And there's good reason when they find themselves trapped in Scareville one dark, haunted night, surrounded by six-foot spiders, zombies and Dr. Fear himself. Will they end up being eaten by Sally the Black Widow? Or will Mike the Zombie's lesson on brains teach them a thing or two about fear?

The Beggar Prince by Brenna McBride
Comedy. 45-55 minutes. 5-12+ females, 2-8+ males (7-20+ performers possible).

When nasty, stuck-up Prince Edmund rudely rejects all of his potential brides-to-be, his frustrated mother Queen Germaine vows to marry him to the next beggar she sees! It's not long before Lil, a most unusual "beggar," arrives and turns Edmund from a prince to a pauper in a matter of minutes. Unbeknownst to both the beggar prince and his new bride, they are about to embark on a remarkable journey and learn some hard-won lessons about kindness, compassion and second chances.

Cuentos de Josefina by Gregory Ramos
Folktale with music. 100-110 minutes. 6+ females, 4+ males (10-50+ performers possible).

A heartfelt memory tale that follows the story of young Josefina and her brother Ignacio's journey from Mexico to the United States after the Mexican revolution. The play explores what it means to leave one land in search of another, and the value in maintaining ties to our past. Based on true Mexican family tales, ***Cuentos de Josefina (Josephine's Tales)*** weaves together a series of stories that can be told with various theatrical devices, including story theatre, movement, music, shadow and puppetry.

Honey's Smile by Robin Rice
Comedy with Music. 35-45 minutes. 2 females, 1 male, 11+ any gender (10-14+ performers possible).

Honey loves her life on Tortola: the plants, the beach, the creatures that live on the land and in the ocean. But Honey's mother plans to move to New York—in the morning. Believing she won't be able to be herself living somewhere other than her beloved Caribbean island, she asks her friends—a wise pelican, a feminist hen, a know-it-all rooster, a trumpet vine and a school of minnows—for help. Can she become a minnow or hen or hide under the vine? Can she jump in a rowboat and float away? What will her friends do without her? And what will her mother do if she can't find Honey?

Roll of Thunder, Hear My Cry by Ed Shockley
Drama. 105-115 minutes. 4+ females, 6+ males (12-40 performers possible).

The gripping story of Cassie Logan's coming of age in Jim Crow Mississippi is brought to life on the stage. A cast of ten principal actors plus an expandable chorus performing in a stark setting transform this epic into an inspiring tale of hope and triumph in the face of adversity.

Made in the USA
Columbia, SC
21 August 2018